VOL. 57

HAL•LEONARD®

GUITAR PLAY-ALONG

AUDIO
ACCESS
INCLUDED

GUNS N' ROSES

PLAYBACK+
Speed • Pitch • Balance • Loop

To access audio visit:
www.halleonard.com/mylibrary

Enter Code
5899-2057-5802-6774

ISBN 978-1-4950-6348-0

HAL•LEONARD®

Visit Hal Leonard Online at
www.halleonard.com

Contact us:
Hal Leonard
7777 West Bluemound Road
Milwaukee, WI 53213
Email: info@halleonard.com

In Europe, contact:
Hal Leonard Europe Limited
42 Wigmore Street
Marylebone, London, W1U 2RN
Email: info@halleonardeurope.com

In Australia, contact:
Hal Leonard Australia Pty. Ltd.
4 Lentara Court
Cheltenham, Victoria, 3192 Australia
Email: info@halleonard.com.au

CONTENTS

GUITAR NOTATION LEGEND

THE MUSICAL STAFF shows pitches and rhythms and is divided by bar lines into measures. Pitches are named after the first seven letters of the alphabet.

TABLATURE graphically represents the guitar fingerboard. Each horizontal line represents a string, and each number represents a fret.

Notes:

Strings:
high E
B
G
D
A
low E

4th string, 2nd fret

1st & 2nd strings open, played together

open D chord

HALF-STEP BEND: Strike the note and bend up 1/2 step.

WHOLE-STEP BEND: Strike the note and bend up one step.

GRACE NOTE BEND: Strike the note and immediately bend up as indicated.

SLIGHT (MICROTONE) BEND: Strike the note and bend up 1/4 step.

BEND AND RELEASE: Strike the note and bend up as indicated, then release back to the original note. Only the first note is struck.

PRE-BEND: Bend the note as indicated, then strike it.

VIBRATO: The string is vibrated by rapidly bending and releasing the note with the fretting hand.

PALM MUTING: The note is partially muted by the pick hand lightly touching the string(s) just before the bridge.

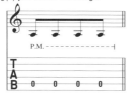

HAMMER-ON: Strike the first (lower) note with one finger, then sound the higher note (on the same string) with another finger by fretting it without picking.

PULL-OFF: Place both fingers on the notes to be sounded. Strike the first note and without picking, pull the finger off to sound the second (lower) note.

LEGATO SLIDE: Strike the first note and then slide the same fret-hand finger up or down to the second note. The second note is not struck.

SHIFT SLIDE: Same as legato slide, except the second note is struck.

TRILL: Very rapidly alternate between the notes indicated by continuously hammering on and pulling off.

TAPPING: Hammer ("tap") the fret indicated with the pick-hand index or middle finger and pull off to the note fretted by the fret hand.

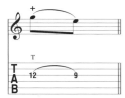

NATURAL HARMONIC: Strike the note while the fret-hand lightly touches the string directly over the fret indicated.

PINCH HARMONIC: The note is fretted normally and a harmonic is produced by adding the edge of the thumb or the tip of the index finger of the pick hand to the normal pick attack.

TREMOLO PICKING: The note is picked as rapidly and continuously as possible.

VIBRATO BAR DIVE AND RETURN: The pitch of the note or chord is dropped a specified number of steps (in rhythm), then returned to the original pitch.

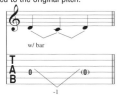

VIBRATO BAR SCOOP: Depress the bar just before striking the note, then quickly release the bar.

VIBRATO BAR DIP: Strike the note and then immediately drop a specified number of steps, then release back to the original pitch.

Additional Musical Definitions

 *(accent)*
- Accentuate note (play it louder).

 *(staccato)*
- Play the note short.

D.S. al Coda
- Go back to the sign (𝄋), then play until the measure marked "***To Coda***," then skip to the section labelled "**Coda**."

D.C. al Fine
- Go back to the beginning of the song and play until the measure marked "***Fine***" (end).

Fill
- Label used to identify a brief melodic figure which is to be inserted into the arrangement.

N.C.
- Harmony is implied.

- Repeat measures between signs.

| 1. | 2. |
- When a repeated section has different endings, play the first ending only the first time and the second ending only the second time.

Don't Cry

Words and Music by Izzy Stradlin' and W. Axl Rose

Tune down 1/2 step:
(low to high) E♭-A♭-D♭-G♭-B♭-E♭

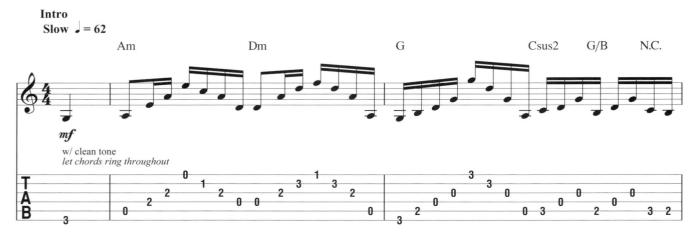

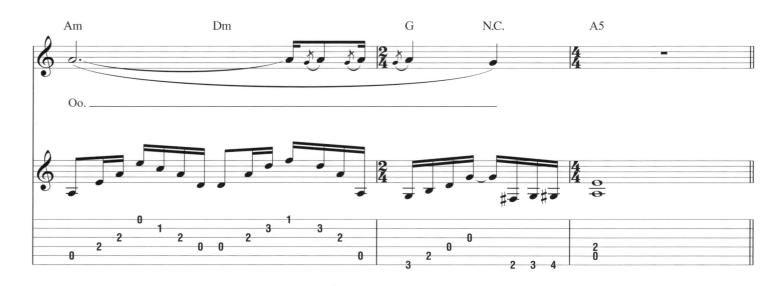

*T = Thumb on 6th string.

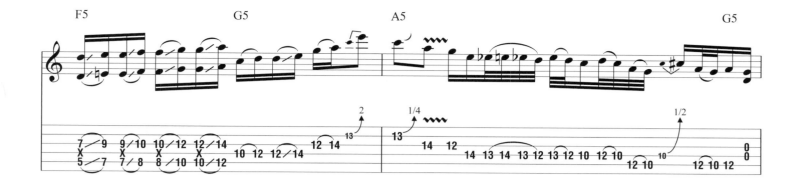

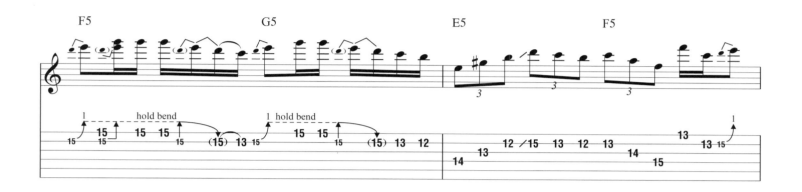

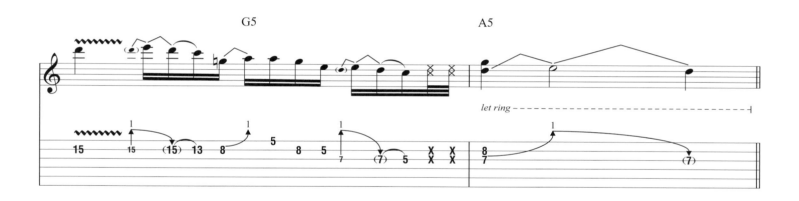

Verse

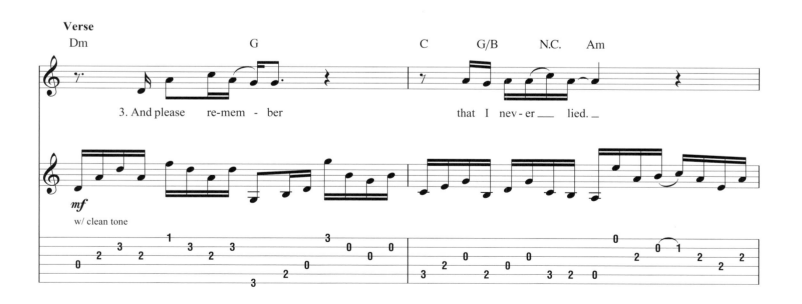

3. And please re-mem - ber that I nev - er ___ lied. ___

Oh, ____ and please _ re-mem - ber how I felt in - side, _ now, hon-ey.

You got - ta _ make _ it your own _ way but you'll be al - right, _ now, sug-ar.

You'll feel _ bet - ter to-mor - row come the morn-ing light, _ now, ba - by.

Chorus

And don't you cry _____ to - night. ____

Patience

Words and Music by W. Axl Rose, Slash, Izzy Stradlin', Duff McKagan and Steven Adler

Tune down 1/2 step:
(low to high) Eb-Ab-Db-Gb-Bb-Eb

Intro
Moderate Rock ♩ = 120
Half-time feel

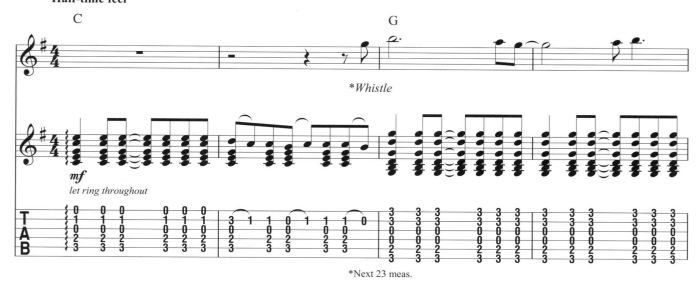

*Whistle

let ring throughout

*Next 23 meas.

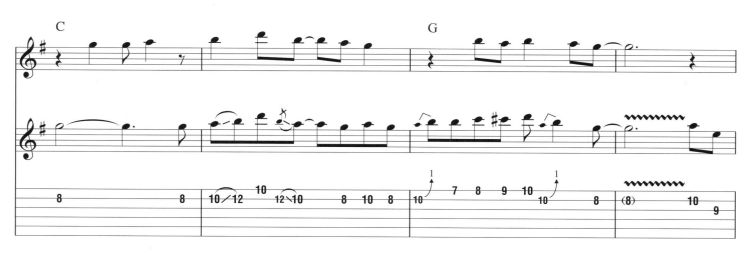

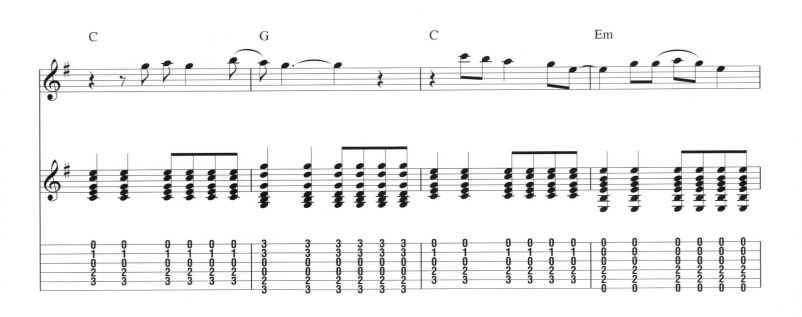

Verse

1. Shed a tear 'cause I'm miss-in' ___ you, ___ I'm still al-right ___ to smile. ___
2. *See additional lyrics*

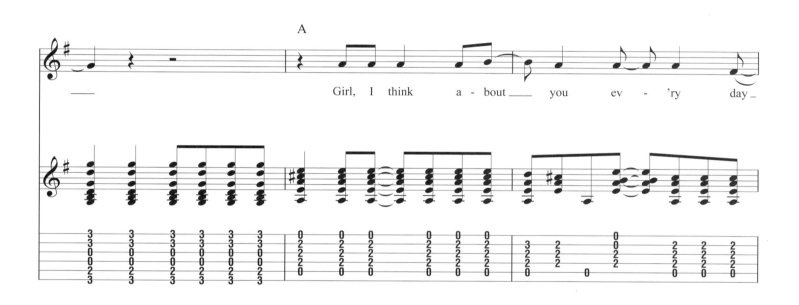

___ Girl, I think a-bout ___ you ev-'ry day ___

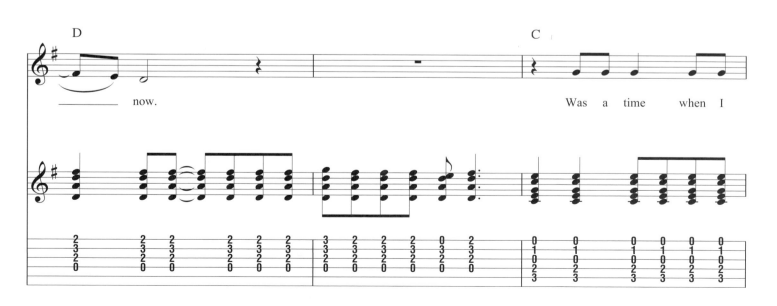

___ now. Was a time when I

was - n't __ sure __ but you set my mind __ at ease. __

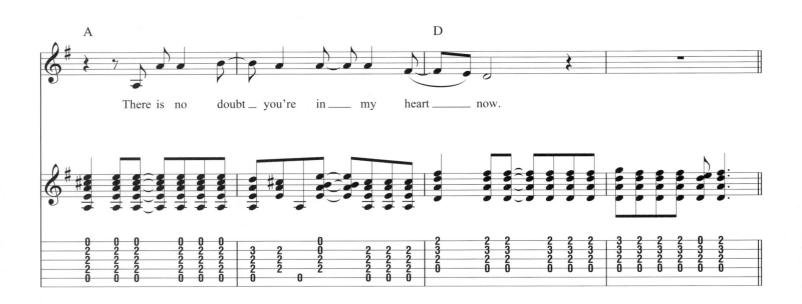

There is no doubt __ you're in __ my heart _____ now.

Chorus

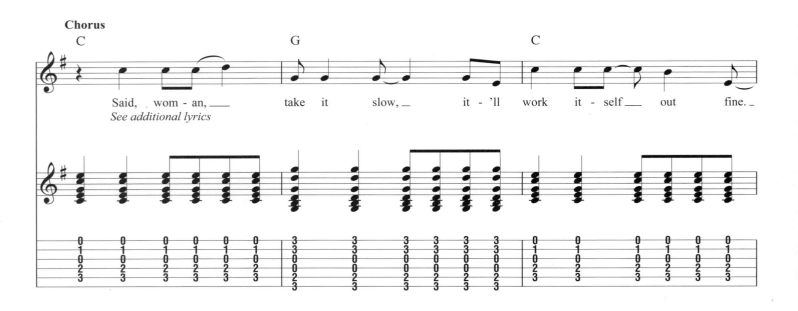

Said, wom - an, __ take it slow, __ it - 'll work it - self __ out fine.
See additional lyrics

All we need ___ is just a lit - tle pa -

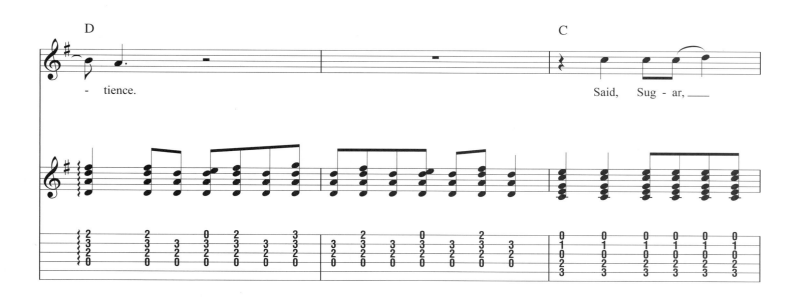

- tience.   Said, Sug - ar, ___

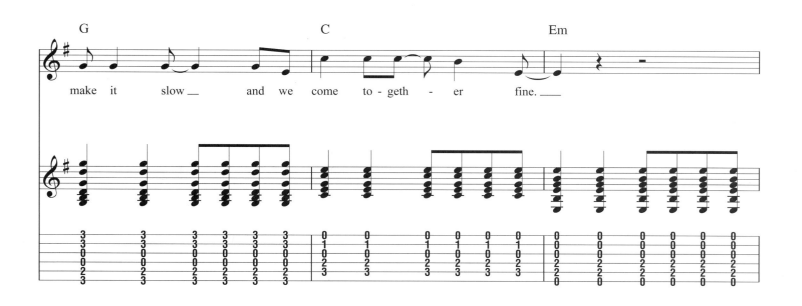

make it slow ___ and we come to - geth - er fine. ___

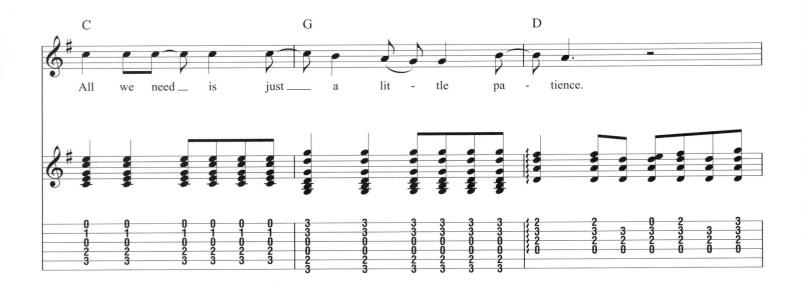

All we need is just a lit - tle pa - tience.

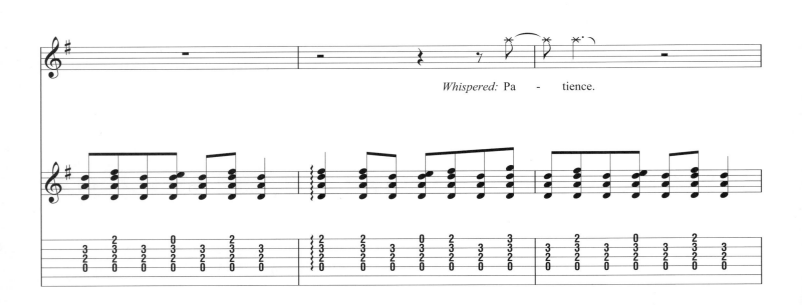

Whispered: Pa - tience.

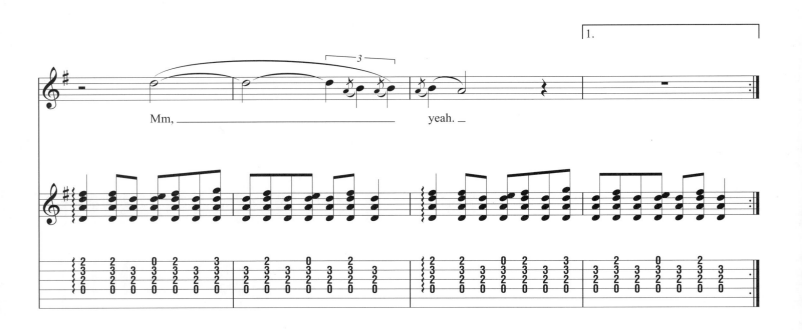

Mm, _____ yeah. _

Guitar Solo

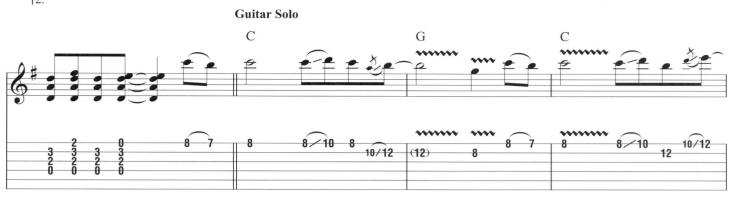

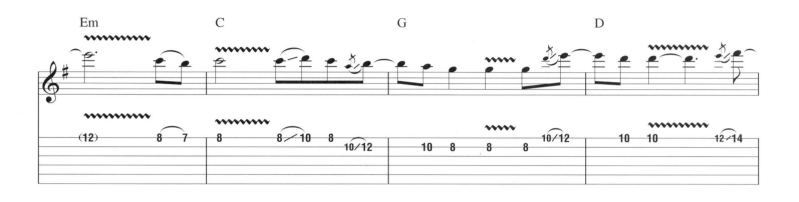

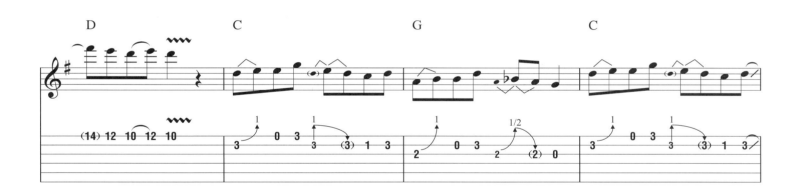

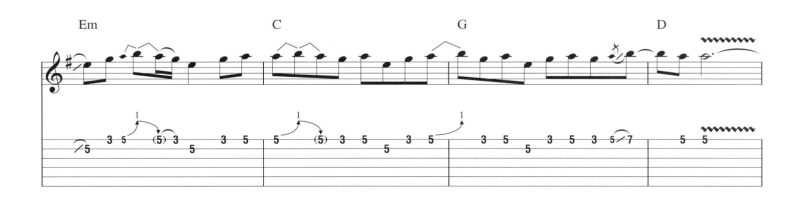

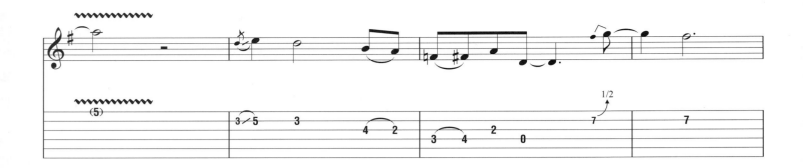

Outro
Slowly ♩ = 64

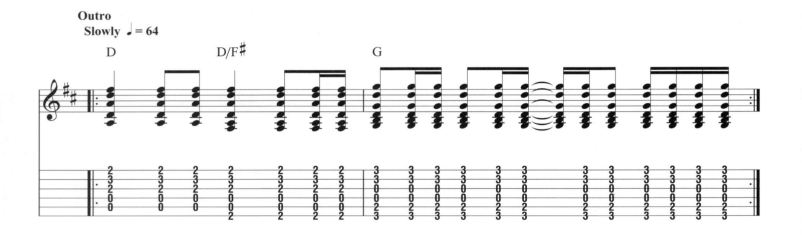

Lit - tle   pa - tience,   mm,   yeah, _____   mm, __

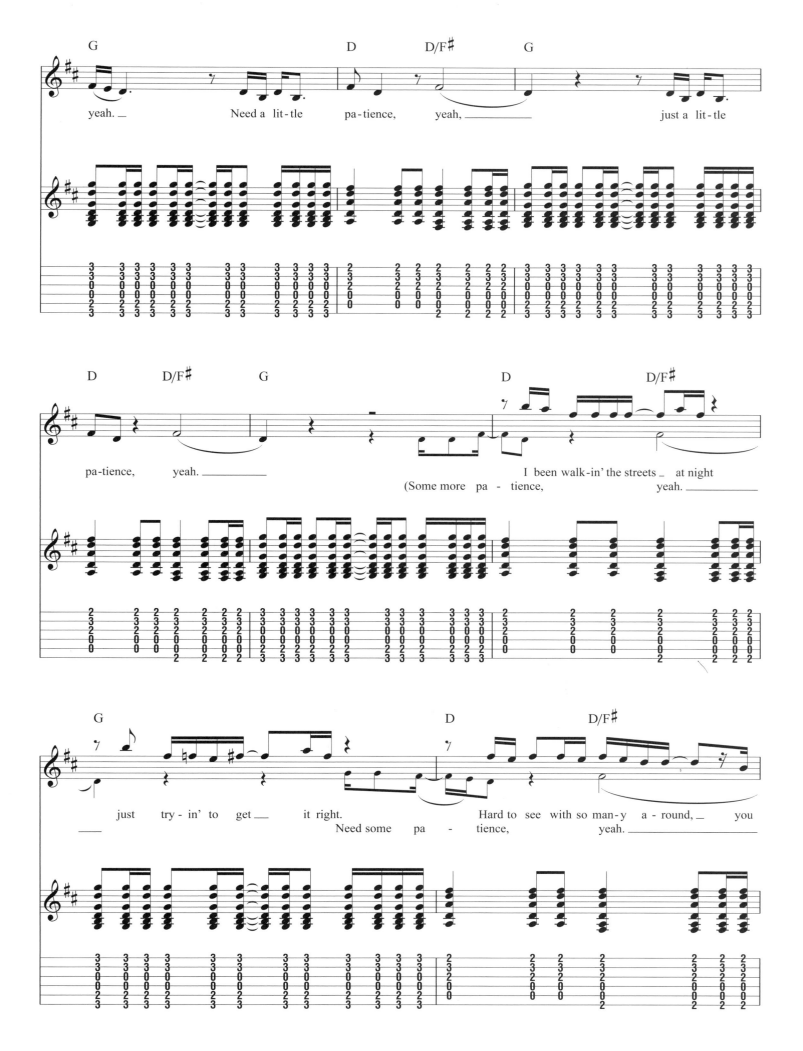

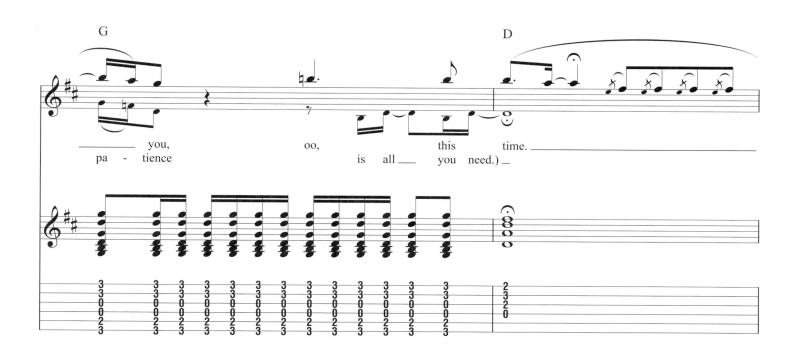

Additional Lyrics

2. I sit here on the stairs 'cause I'd rather be alone.
   If I can't have you right now I'll wait, dear.
   Sometimes I get so tense but I can't speed up the time.
   But you know, love, there's one more thing to consider.

Chorus Said, woman, take it slow and things will be just fine.
   You and I'll just use a little patience.
   Said, Sugar, take the time 'cause the lights are shining bright.
   You and I've got what it takes to make it.
   We won't fake it, ah, I'll never break it 'cause I can't take it.

It's So Easy

**Words and Music by W. Axl Rose, Slash, Izzy Stradlin',
Duff McKagan, Steven Adler and Aaron West Arkeen**

Tune down 1/2 step:
(low to high) E♭-A♭-D♭-G♭-B♭-E♭

Intro
Moderately ♩ = 152

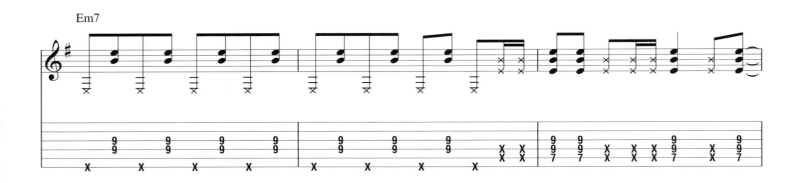

Verse

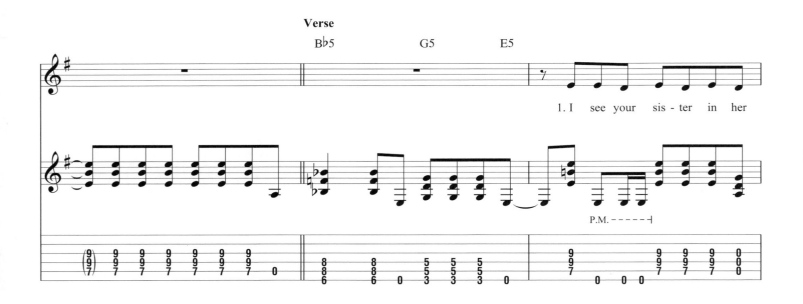

1. I see your sis-ter in her

*Allow 3rd string to be caught under bend finger.

Outro-Guitar Solo

Mr. Brownstone

Words and Music by W. Axl Rose, Slash, Izzy Stradlin', Duff McKagan and Steven Adler

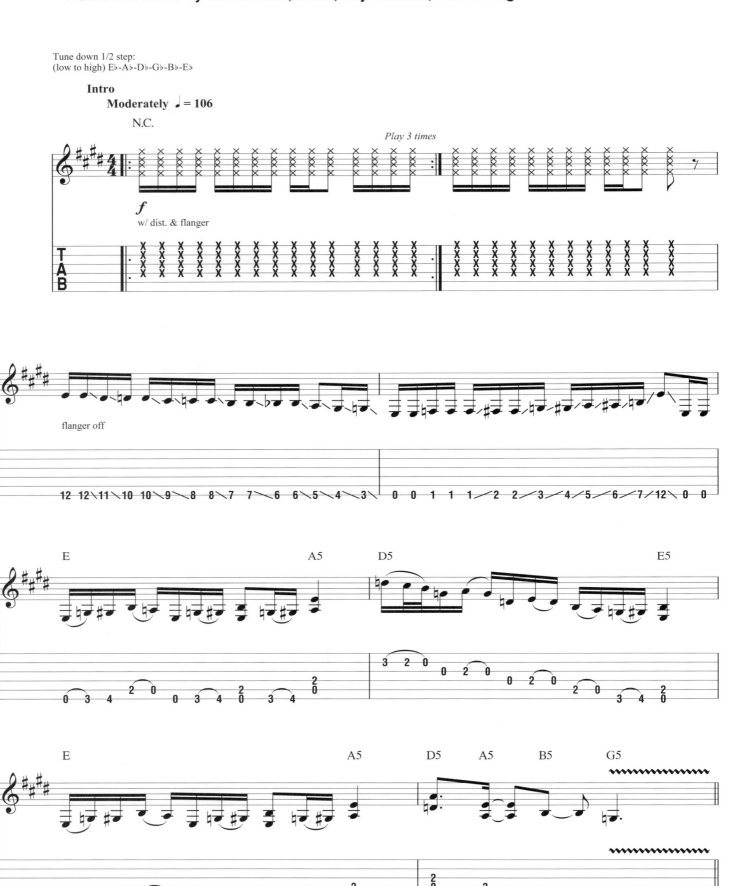

Guitar Solo

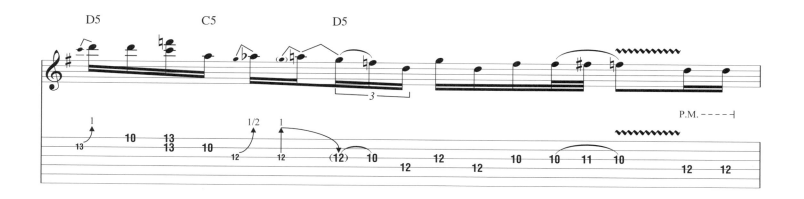

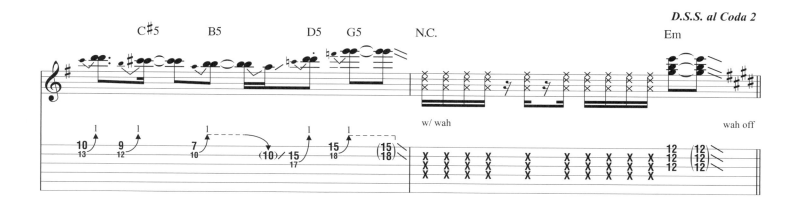

⊕ Coda 2

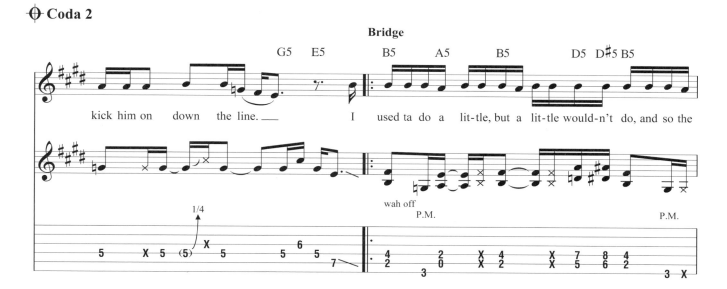

Outro

Stuck it in the mid-dle, and I shot it in the mid-dle, and it, it drove me out-ta my mind. ___ I

slight P.M.

P.H. (8va)

should-a known bet-ter, said I wish I nev-er met her, said I, I leave it all be-hind. _____

let ring

Free time

Yow - za!

let ring

Additional Lyrics

2. Show usually starts around seven; we go on stage around nine.
   Get on the bus about eleven, sippin' a drink and feelin' fine.

3. Now I get up around whenever; I used ta get up on time.
   But that old man, he's a real muthafucker; gonna kick him on down the line.

Nightrain

Words and Music by W. Axl Rose, Slash, Izzy Stradlin', Duff McKagan and Steven Adler

Tune down 1/2 step:
(low to high) Eb-Ab-Db-Gb-Bb-Eb

Intro
Moderately fast ♩ = 150

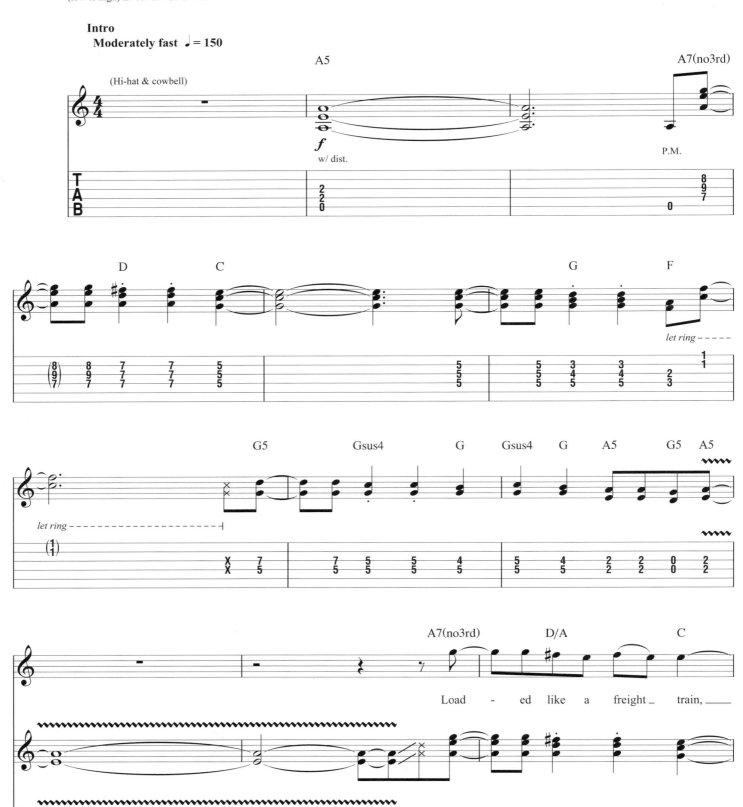

Load - ed like a freight _ train, ____

Read-y to crash and burn._____ I nev-er learn.___ I'm on the night-train. I love that stuff._ I'm on the night-train,_____ and I can nev-er get e-nough. I'm on the night-train, nev-er to___ re-turn._

No!

Guitar Solo

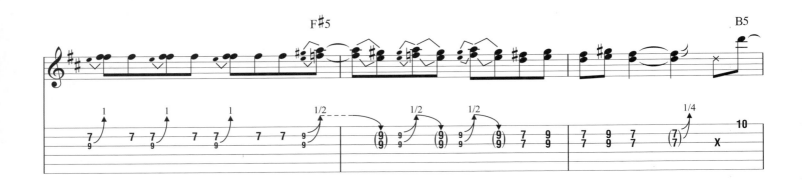

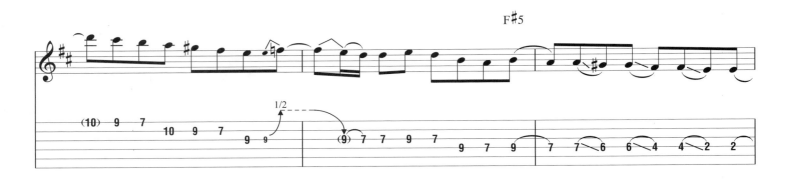

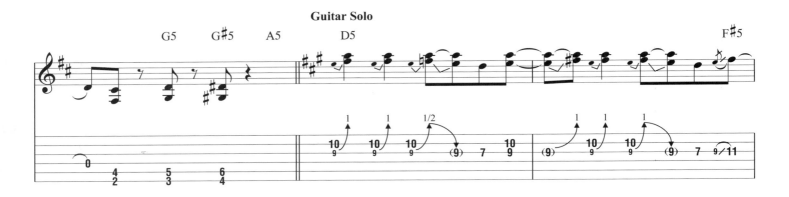

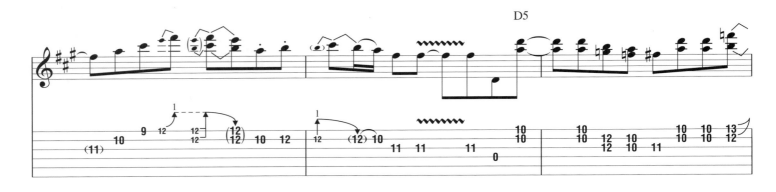

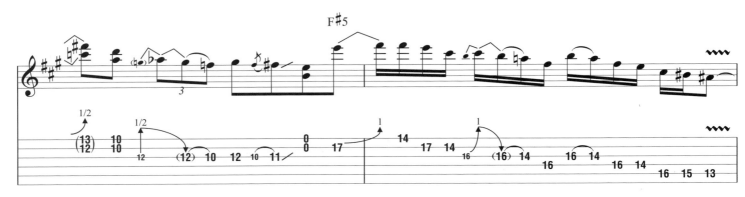

night - train, _____ nev - er to _____ re - turn, _____

yeah. __

Outro-Guitar Solo

Night - train.

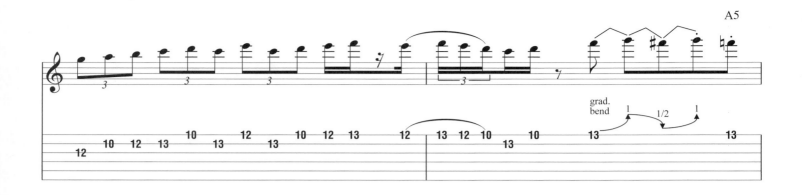

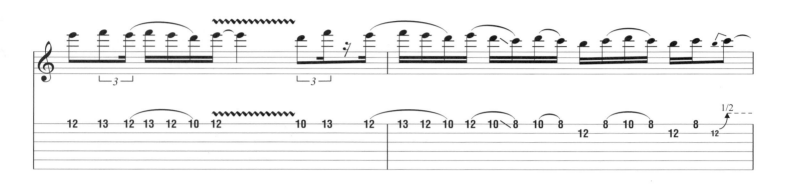

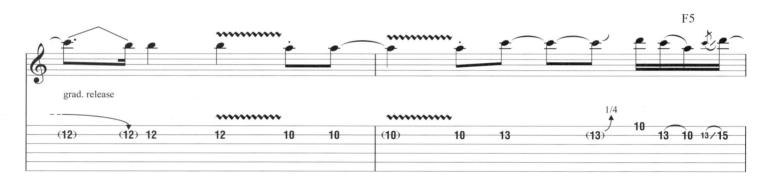

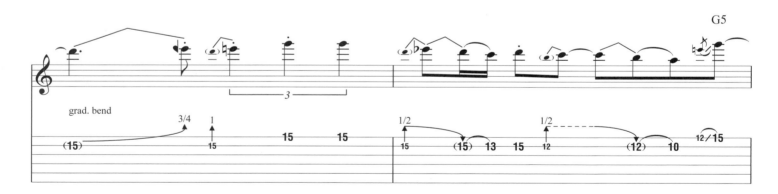

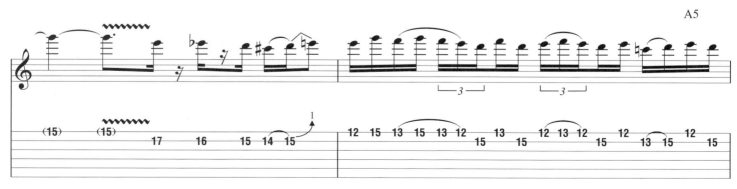

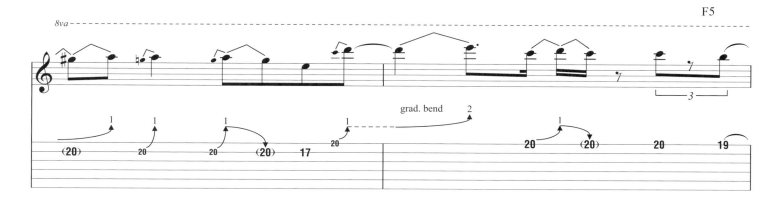

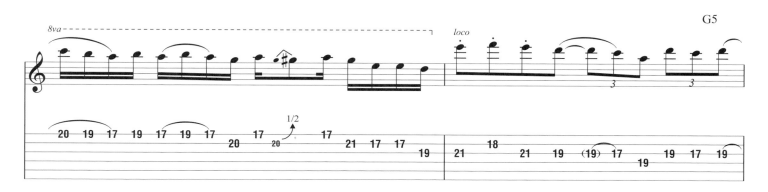

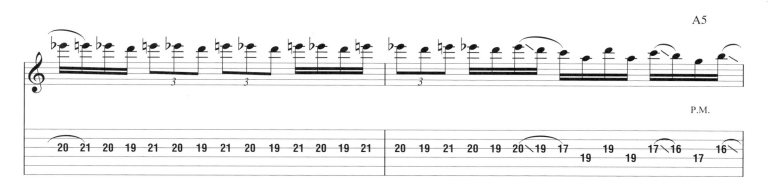

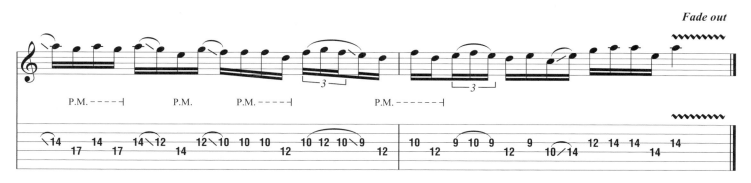

Sweet Child O' Mine

Words and Music by W. Axl Rose, Slash, Izzy Stradlin', Duff McKagan and Steven Adler

Tune down 1/2 step:
(low to high) E♭-A♭-D♭-G♭-B♭-E♭

Intro
Moderate Rock ♩ = 122

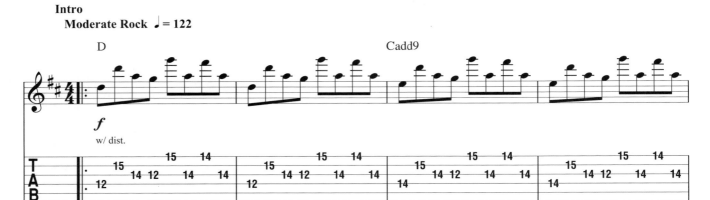

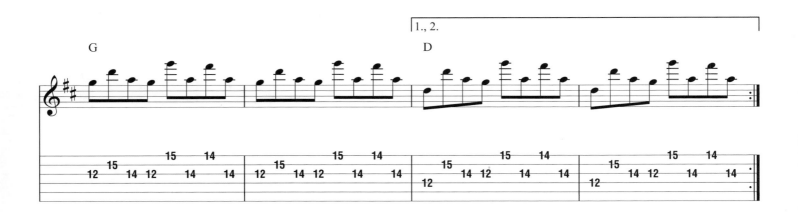

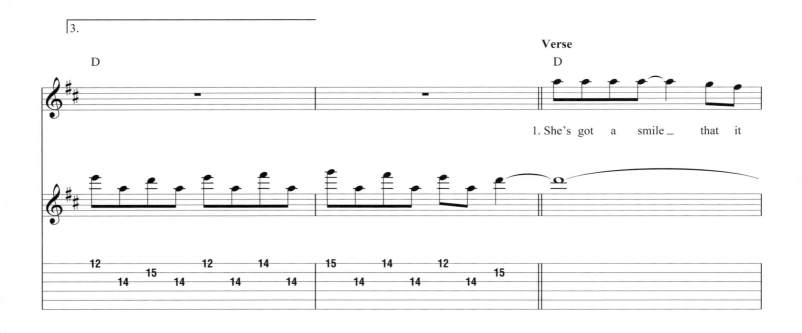

1. She's got a smile ___ that it

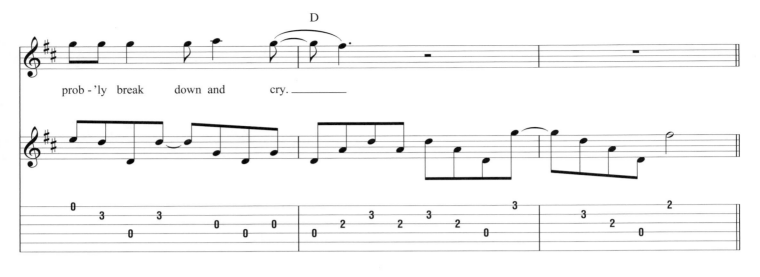

prob -'ly break down and cry. ____

Chorus

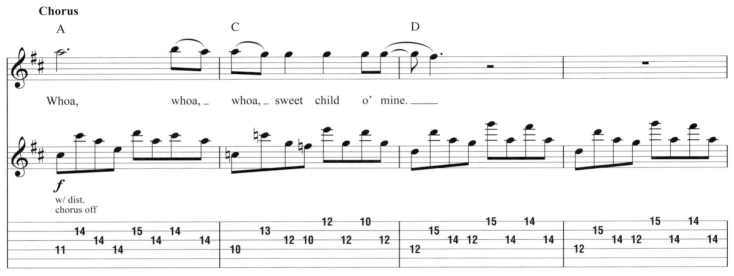

Whoa, whoa, _ whoa, _ sweet child o' mine. ____

w/ dist.
chorus off

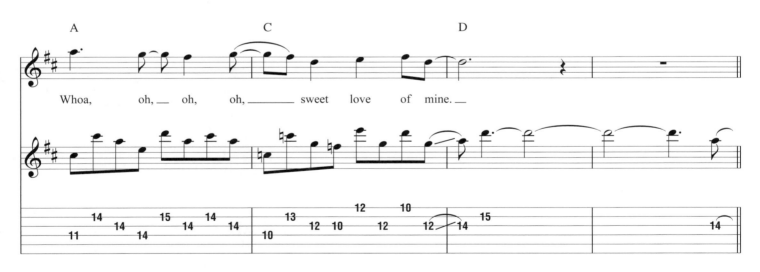

Whoa, oh, __ oh, oh, _____ sweet love of mine. __

Guitar Solo

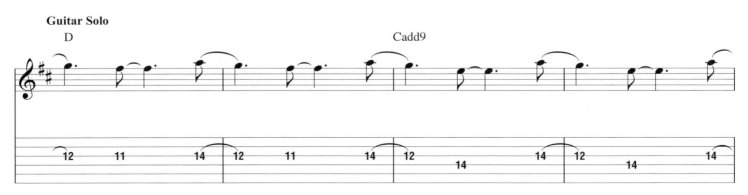

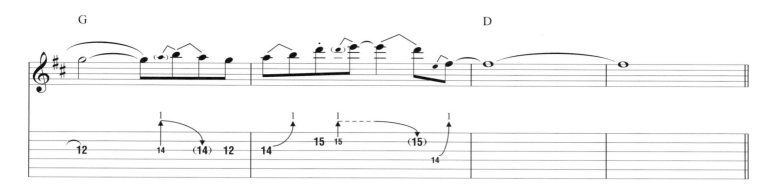

Verse

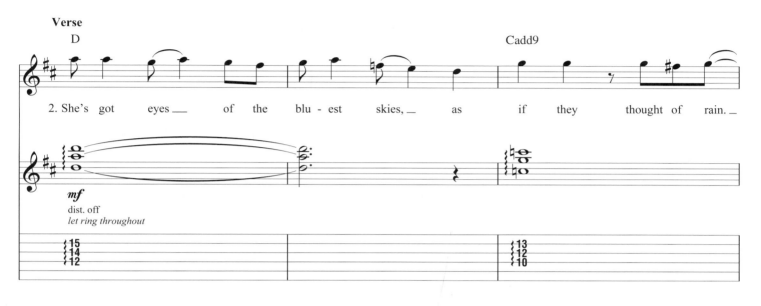

2. She's got eyes ___ of the blu - est skies, ___ as if they thought of rain. ___

mf
dist. off
let ring throughout

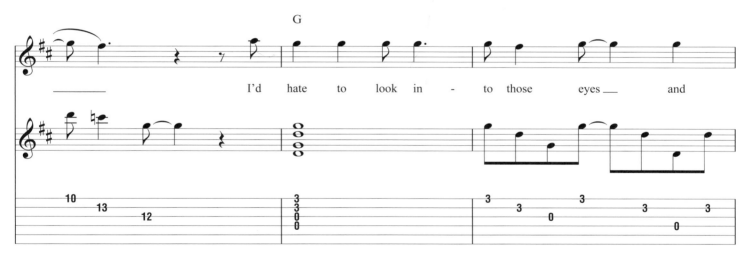

___ I'd hate to look in - to those eyes ___ and

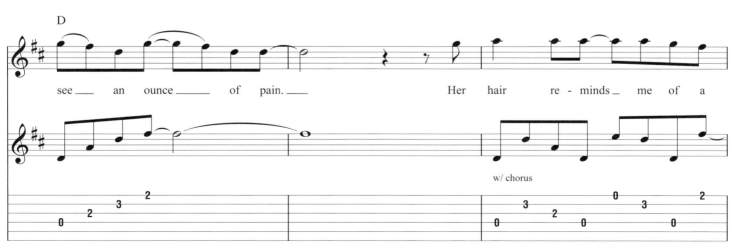

see ___ an ounce ___ of pain. ___ Her hair re - minds ___ me of a

w/ chorus

Oo, ___ yeah, ah! ___ Ooh, ___

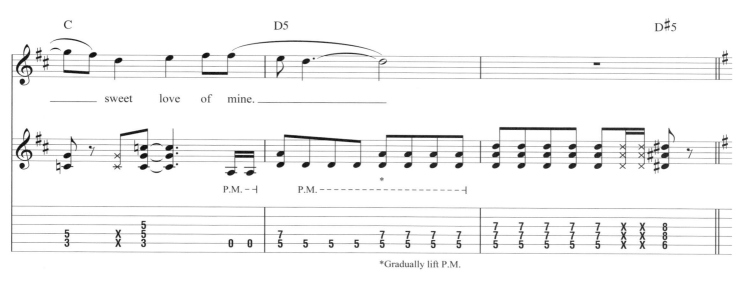

___ sweet love of mine. ___

*Gradually lift P.M.

Guitar Solo

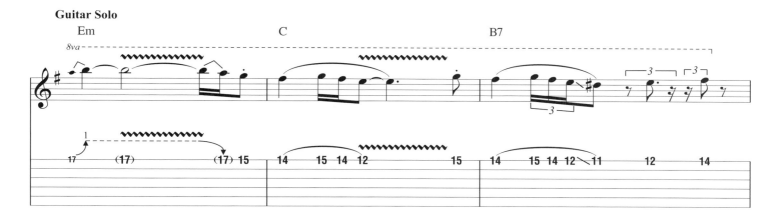

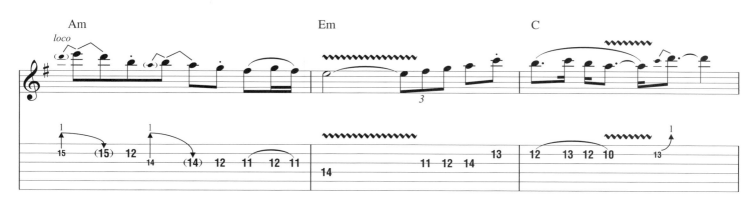

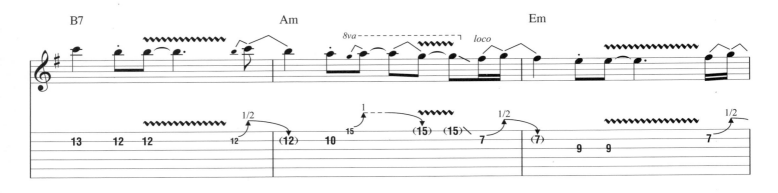

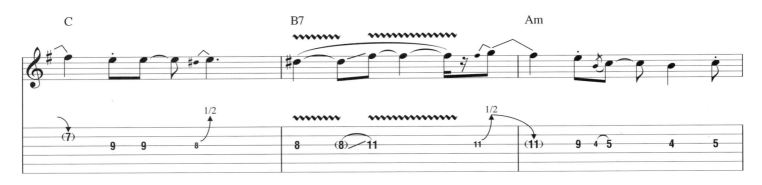

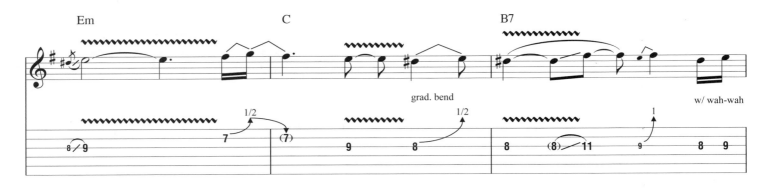

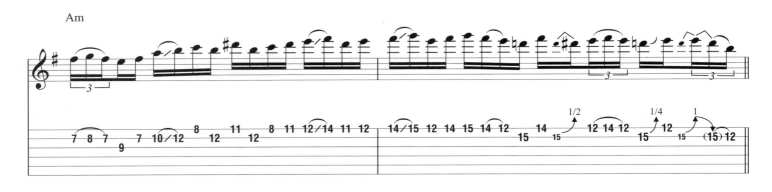

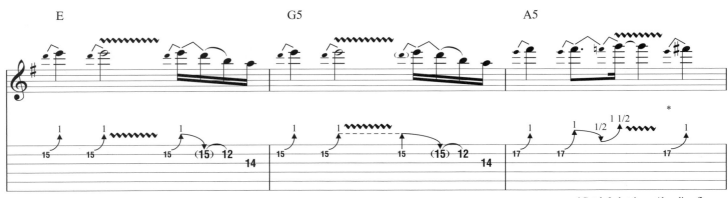

*Catch 3rd string w/ bending finger.

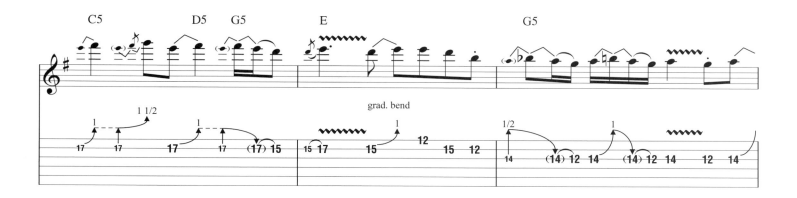

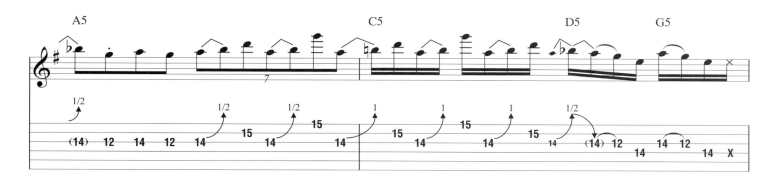

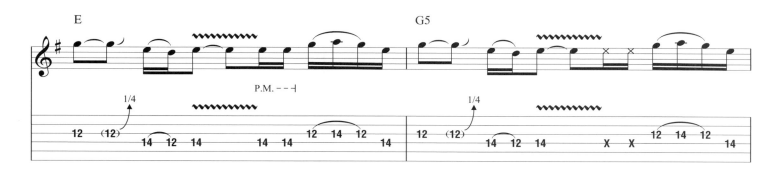

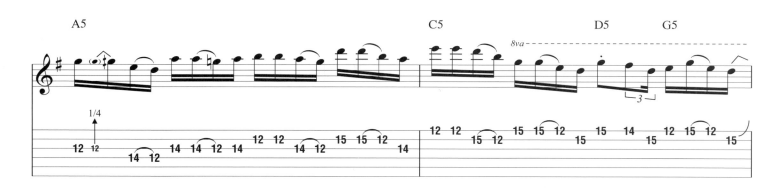

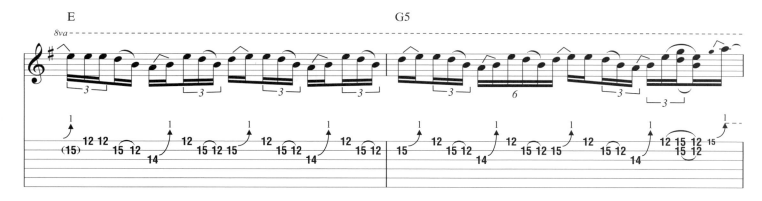

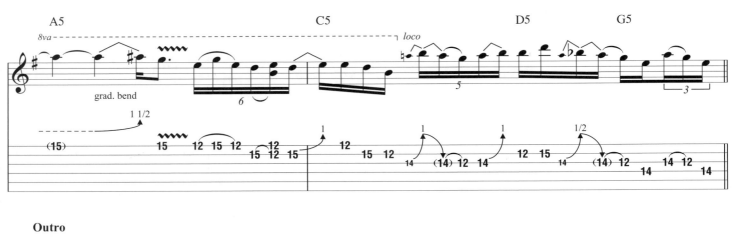

Outro

Where do we go? — Where do we go — now? Where do we go? —

Mm, — mm, — oh. — Where do we go? _____ Oh. —

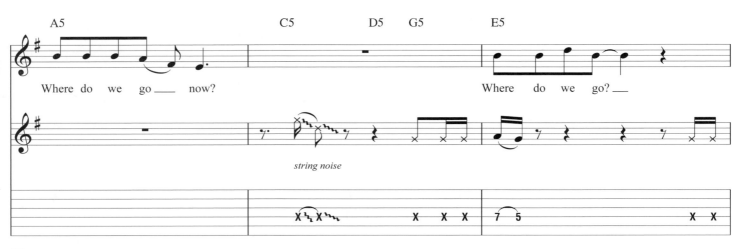

Where do we go ___ now? Where do we go? —

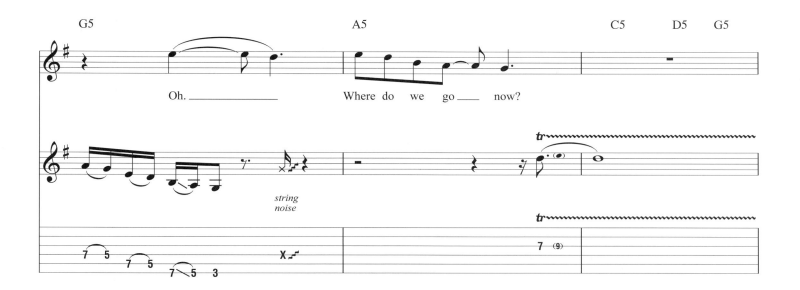

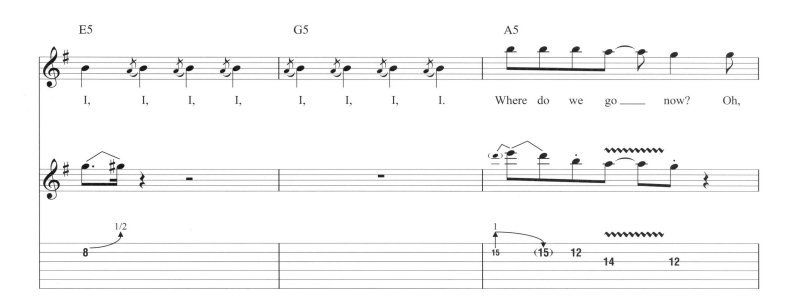

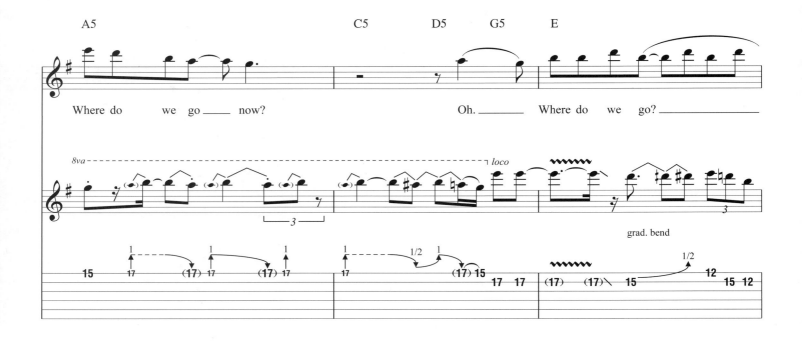

Where do we go ___ now?   Oh. ___ Where do we go? ___

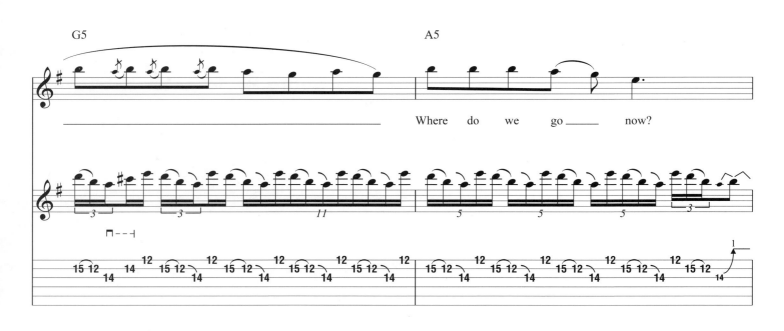

___   Where do we go ___ now?

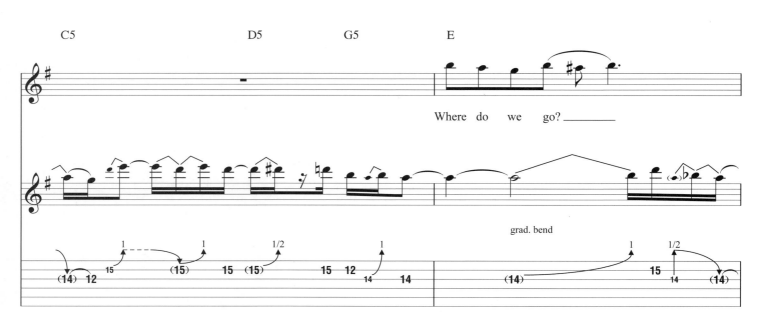

Where do we go? ___

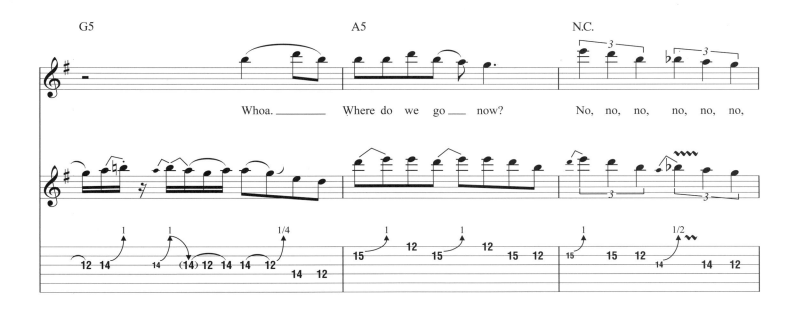

Whoa. _____ Where do we go _____ now?   No, no, no,   no, no, no,

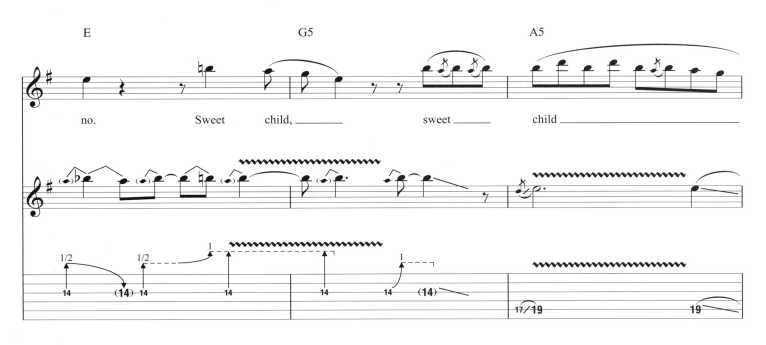

no.   Sweet   child, _____   sweet _____   child _____

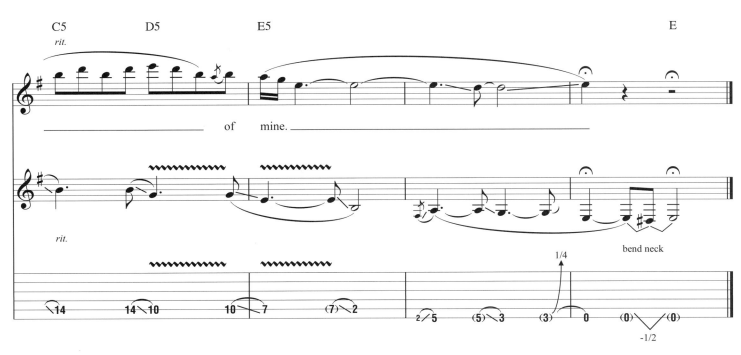

_____ of   mine. _____

Used to Love Her

Words and Music by W. Axl Rose, Slash, Izzy Stradlin', Duff McKagan and Steven Adler

Tune down 1/2 step:
(low to high) E♭-A♭-D♭-G♭-B♭-E♭

Intro
Moderately fast ♩ = 135

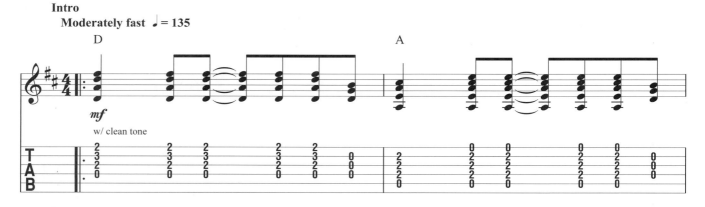

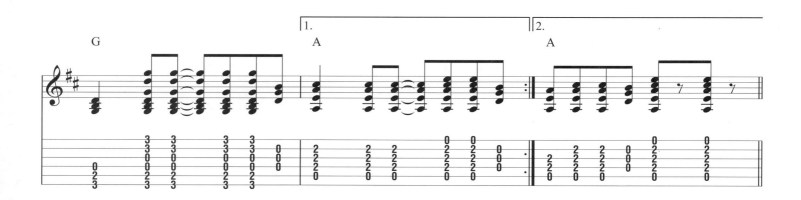

Verse

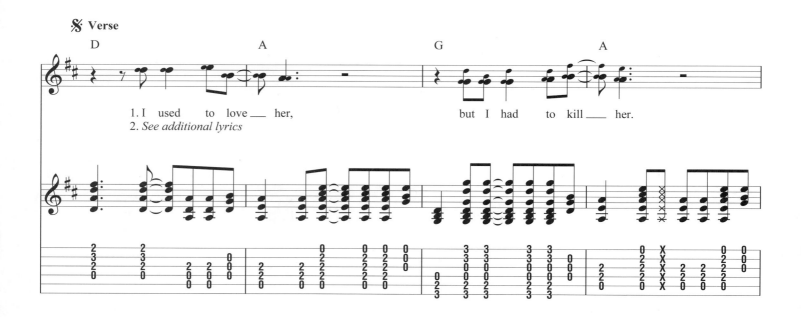

1. I used to love ___ her, but I had to kill ___ her.
2. *See additional lyrics*

I used to love __ her, oo, _____ yeah, but I had to kill __ her.

To Coda ⊕

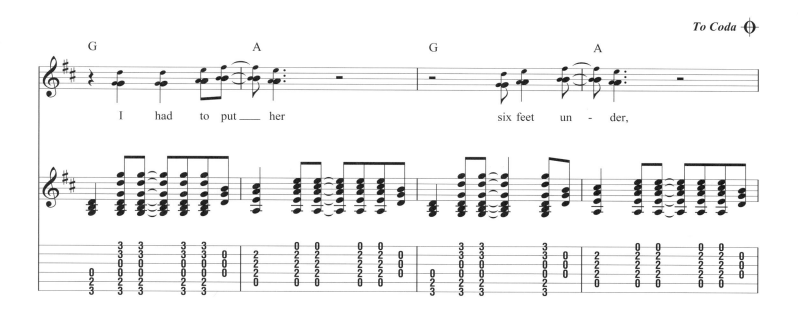

I had to put __ her six feet un - der,

D.S. al Coda

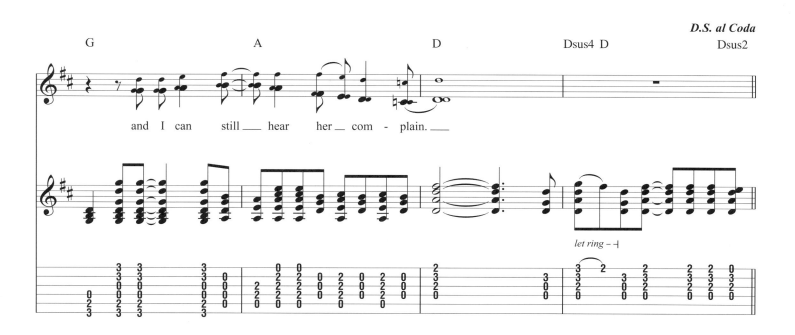

and I can still __ hear her __ com - plain. __

let ring

Coda

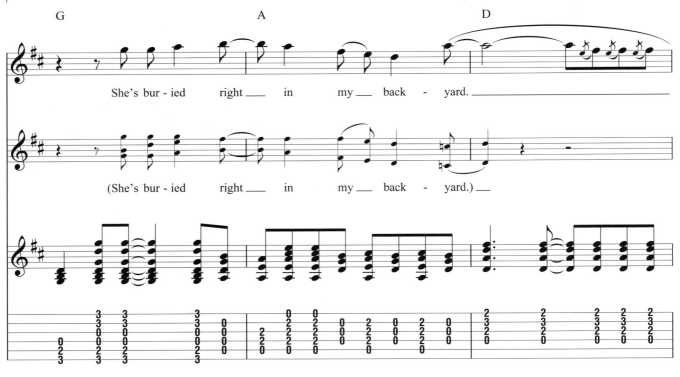

She's bur - ied right ___ in ___ my ___ back - yard. ___

(She's bur - ied right ___ in ___ my ___ back - yard.) ___

Guitar Solo

_____ Oh, ___ oh, ___ yeah. Oo, _____ yeah. __

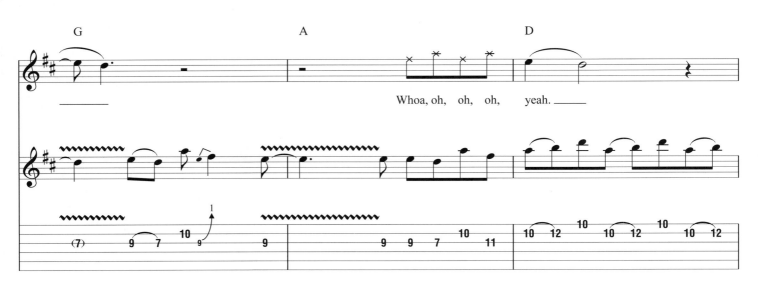

_____ Whoa, oh, oh, oh, yeah. ___

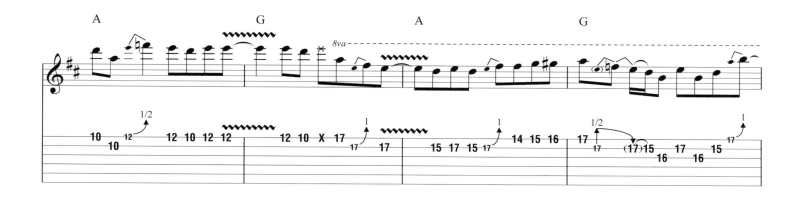

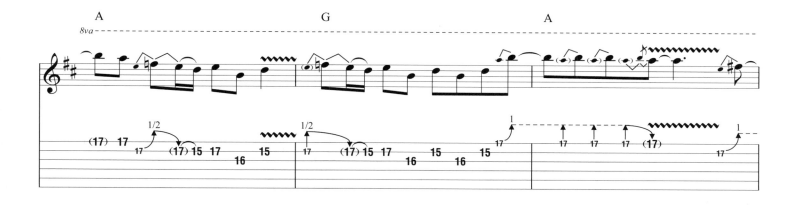

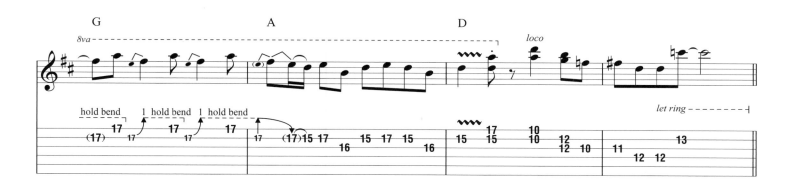

Verse

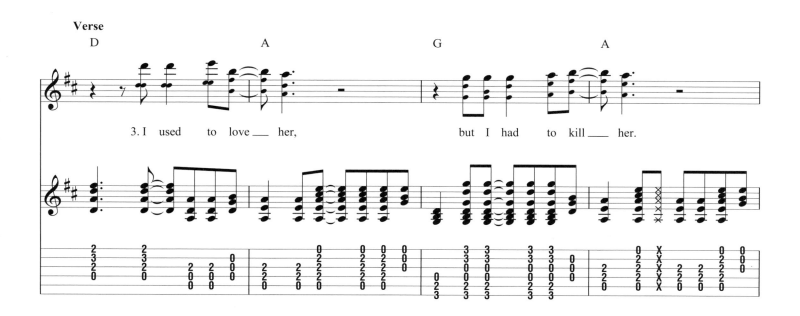

3. I used to love ___ her, but I had to kill ___ her.

Guitar Solo

Whoa, _ oh, _ yeah.

Spoken: Take it for what it

is.

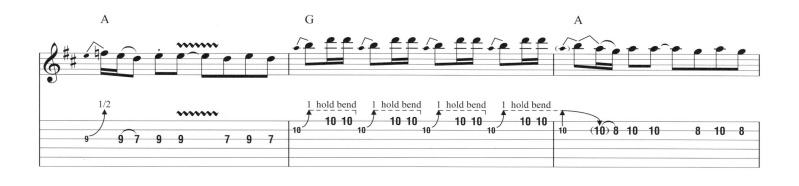

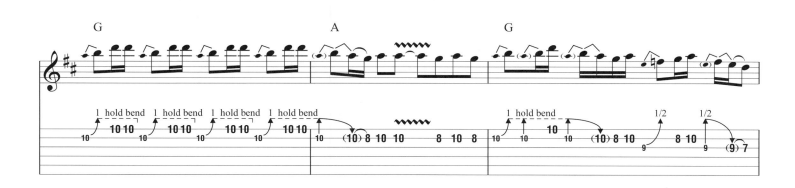

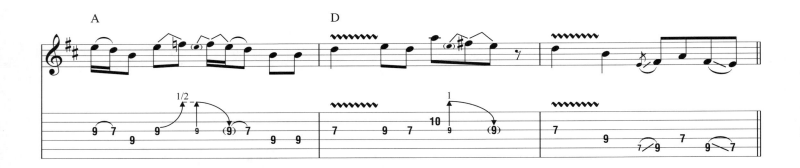

Verse

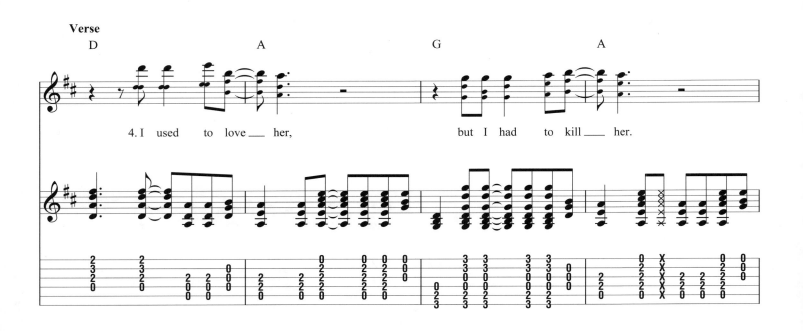

4. I used to love ___ her,   but I had to kill ___ her.

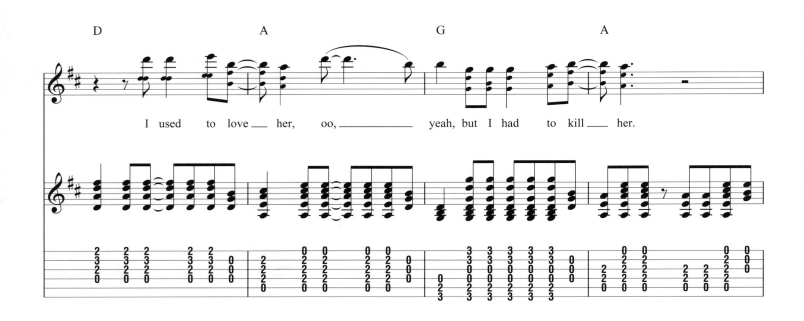

I used to love ___ her, oo, ___ yeah, but I had to kill ___ her.

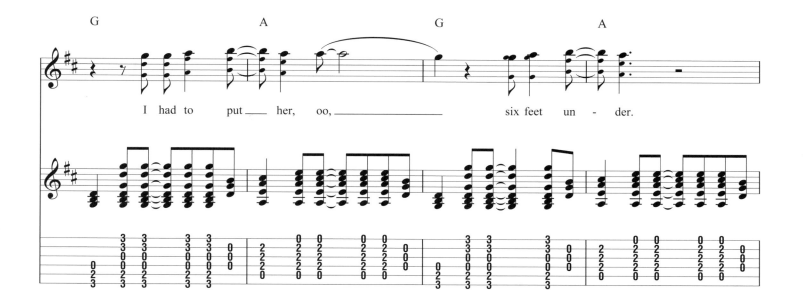

I had to put ___ her, oo, ___ six feet un - der.

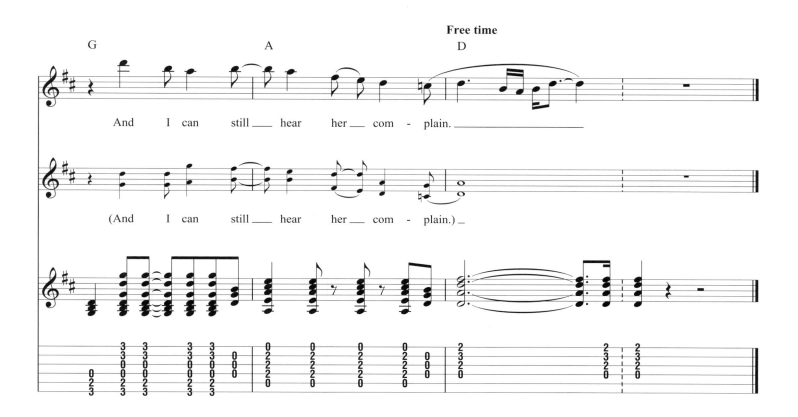

And I can still ___ hear her ___ com - plain. ___

(And I can still ___ hear her ___ com - plain.) ___

Additional Lyrics

2. I used to love her, oo, yeah,
But I had to kill her.
I used to love her, oo, yeah,
But I had to kill her.
I knew I'd miss her,
So I had to keep her.
She's buried right in my backyard.

Rocket Queen

Words and Music by W. Axl Rose, Slash, Izzy Stradlin', Duff McKagan and Steven Adler

Tune down 1/2 step:
(low to high) Eb-Ab-Db-Gb-Bb-Eb

Intro
Moderately ♩ = 114

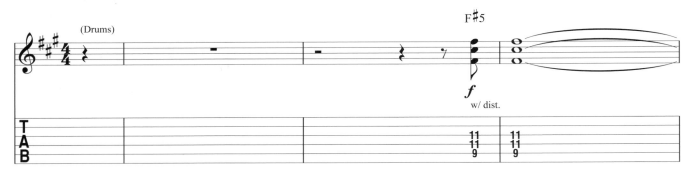

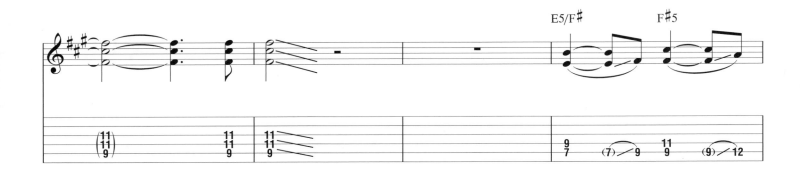

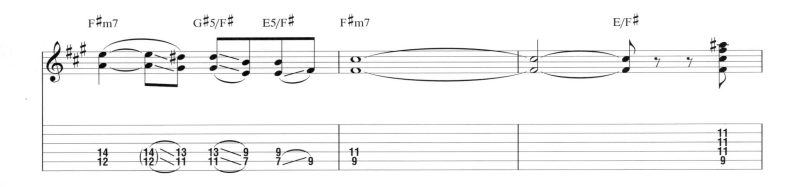

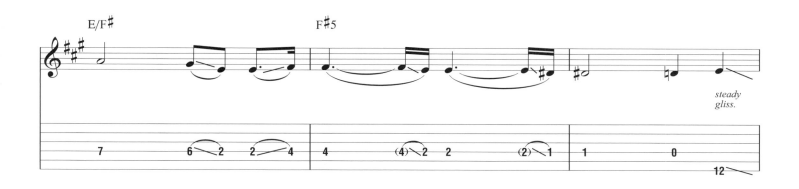

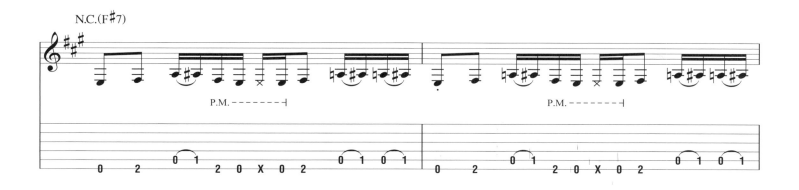

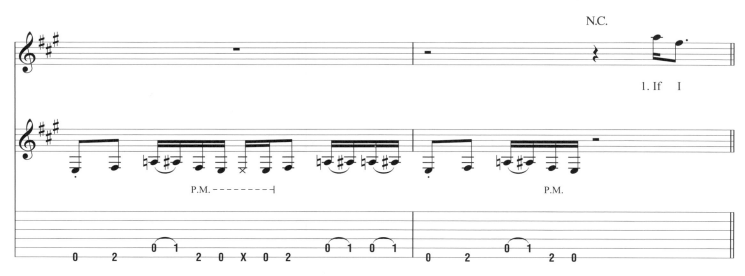

Verse

say I don't_ need an-y-one,_ I can say these things to you._ 'Cause

I can turn on an-y-one_ just like I've turned on you. I've got a

tongue like a ra - zor, a sweet switch-blade knife. And

I can do you fa - vors, but then you'll do what-ev - er I like. Here I am,_

Chorus

2nd & 3rd times, substitute Fill 1

... and you're a rock-et queen. ___ I might

be a lit-tle young, but hon-ey, I ain't na-ive. ___ Here I am, ___

... and you're a rock-et queen, oh, yeah. ___ I might

Fill 1

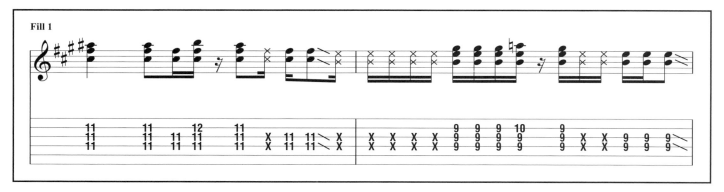

be   too much, but hon - ey, you're a bit ob - scene._____

Interlude

2. I've seen

⊕ Coda 1

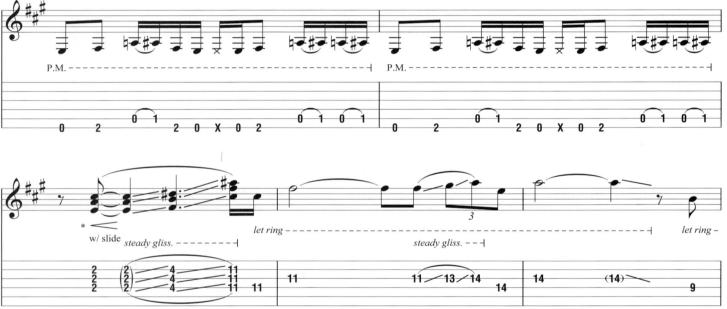

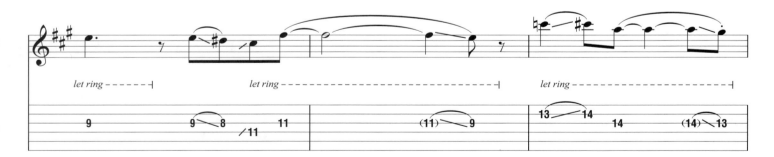

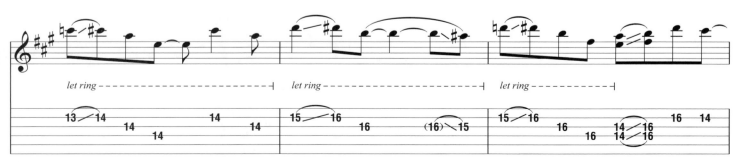

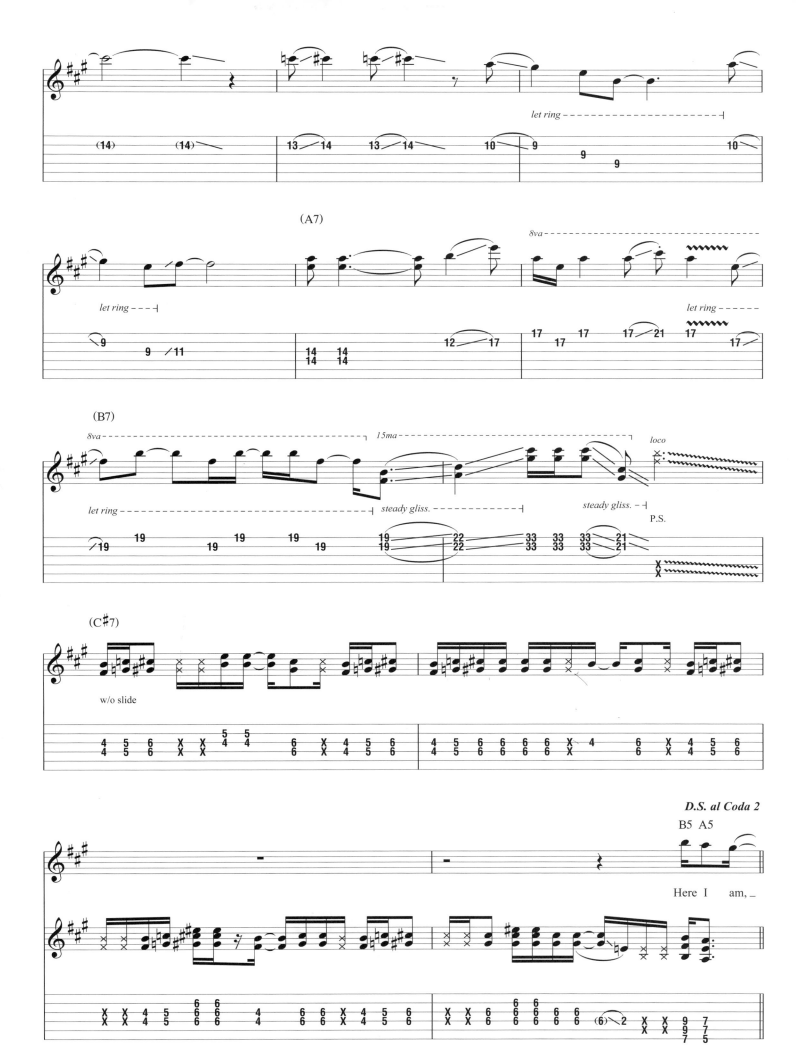

Coda 2

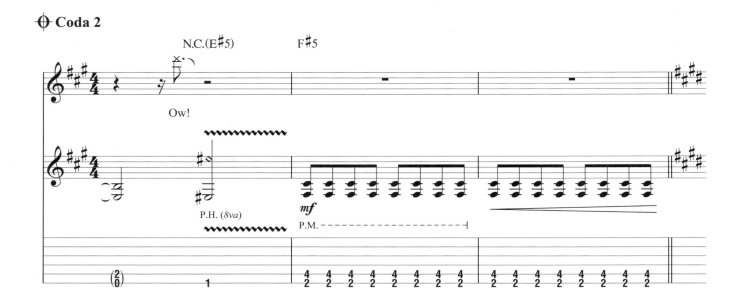

Interlude

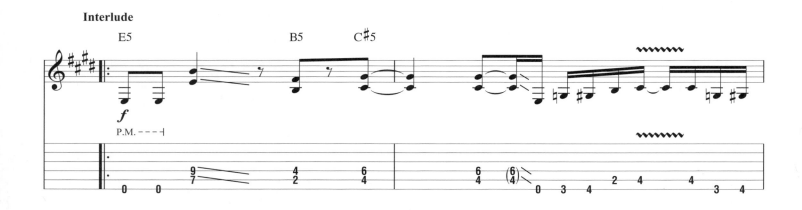

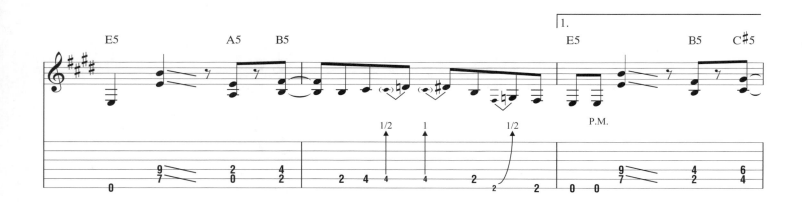

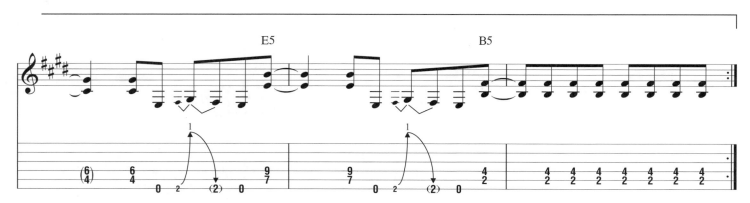

*Increase vol. knob to 10.

HAL•LEONARD GUITAR PLAY-ALONG

Complete song lists available online.

This series will help you play your favorite songs quickly and easily. Just follow the tab and listen to the audio to the hear how the guitar should sound, and then play along using the separate backing tracks. Audio files also include software to slow down the tempo without changing pitch. The melody and lyrics are included in the book so that you can sing or simply follow along.

INCLUDES TAB

VOL. 1 – ROCK .... 00699570 / $16.99
VOL. 2 – ACOUSTIC .... 00699569 / $16.99
VOL. 3 – HARD ROCK .... 00699573 / $17.99
VOL. 4 – POP/ROCK .... 00699571 / $16.99
VOL. 5 – THREE CHORD SONGS .... 00300985 / $16.99
VOL. 6 – '90S ROCK .... 00298615 / $16.99
VOL. 7 – BLUES .... 00699575 / $17.99
VOL. 8 – ROCK .... 00699585 / $16.99
VOL. 9 – EASY ACOUSTIC SONGS .... 00151708 / $16.99
VOL. 10 – ACOUSTIC .... 00699586 / $16.95
VOL. 11 – EARLY ROCK .... 00699579 / $15.99
VOL. 12 – ROCK POP .... 00291724 / $16.99
VOL. 14 – BLUES ROCK .... 00699582 / $16.99
VOL. 15 – R&B .... 00699583 / $17.99
VOL. 16 – JAZZ .... 00699584 / $15.95
VOL. 17 – COUNTRY .... 00699588 / $16.99
VOL. 18 – ACOUSTIC ROCK .... 00699577 / $15.95
VOL. 20 – ROCKABILLY .... 00699580 / $16.99
VOL. 21 – SANTANA .... 00174525 / $17.99
VOL. 22 – CHRISTMAS .... 00699600 / $15.99
VOL. 23 – SURF .... 00699635 / $16.99
VOL. 24 – ERIC CLAPTON .... 00699649 / $17.99
VOL. 25 – THE BEATLES .... 00198265 / $17.99
VOL. 26 – ELVIS PRESLEY .... 00699643 / $16.99
VOL. 27 – DAVID LEE ROTH .... 00699645 / $16.95
VOL. 28 – GREG KOCH .... 00699646 / $17.99
VOL. 29 – BOB SEGER .... 00699647 / $16.99
VOL. 30 – KISS .... 00699644 / $16.99
VOL. 32 – THE OFFSPRING .... 00699653 / $14.95
VOL. 33 – ACOUSTIC CLASSICS .... 00699656 / $17.99
VOL. 34 – CLASSIC ROCK .... 00699658 / $17.99
VOL. 35 – HAIR METAL .... 00699660 / $17.99
VOL. 36 – SOUTHERN ROCK .... 00699661 / $19.99
VOL. 37 – ACOUSTIC UNPLUGGED .... 00699662 / $22.99
VOL. 38 – BLUES .... 00699663 / $17.99
VOL. 39 – '80s METAL .... 00699664 / $16.99
VOL. 40 – INCUBUS .... 00699668 / $17.95
VOL. 41 – ERIC CLAPTON .... 00699669 / $17.99
VOL. 42 – COVER BAND HITS .... 00211597 / $16.99
VOL. 43 – LYNYRD SKYNYRD .... 00699681 / $19.99
VOL. 44 – JAZZ GREATS .... 00699689 / $16.99
VOL. 45 – TV THEMES .... 00699718 / $14.95
VOL. 46 – MAINSTREAM ROCK .... 00699722 / $16.95
VOL. 47 – JIMI HENDRIX SMASH HITS .... 00699723 / $19.99
VOL. 48 – AEROSMITH CLASSICS .... 00699724 / $17.99
VOL. 49 – STEVIE RAY VAUGHAN .... 00699725 / $17.99
VOL. 50 – VAN HALEN: 1978-1984 .... 00110269 / $19.99
VOL. 51 – ALTERNATIVE '90s .... 00699727 / $14.99
VOL. 52 – FUNK .... 00699728 / $15.99
VOL. 53 – DISCO .... 00699729 / $14.99
VOL. 54 – HEAVY METAL .... 00699730 / $16.99
VOL. 55 – POP METAL .... 00699731 / $14.95
VOL. 56 – FOO FIGHTERS .... 00699749 / $17.99
VOL. 57 – GUNS 'N' ROSES .... 00159922 / $17.99
VOL. 58 – BLINK 182 .... 00699772 / $14.95
VOL. 59 – CHET ATKINS .... 00702347 / $16.99
VOL. 60 – 3 DOORS DOWN .... 00699774 / $14.95
VOL. 62 – CHRISTMAS CAROLS .... 00699798 / $12.95
VOL. 63 – CREEDENCE CLEARWATER
        REVIVAL .... 00699802 / $16.99
VOL. 64 – ULTIMATE OZZY OSBOURNE .... 00699803 / $17.99
VOL. 66 – THE ROLLING STONES .... 00699807 / $17.99
VOL. 67 – BLACK SABBATH .... 00699808 / $16.99
VOL. 68 – PINK FLOYD –
        DARK SIDE OF THE MOON .... 00699809 / $16.99
VOL. 71 – CHRISTIAN ROCK .... 00699824 / $14.95

VOL. 72 – ACOUSTIC '90s .... 00699827 / $14.95
VOL. 73 – BLUESY ROCK .... 00699829 / $16.99
VOL. 74 – SIMPLE STRUMMING SONGS .. 00151706 / $19.99
VOL. 75 – TOM PETTY .... 00699882 / $17.99
VOL. 76 – COUNTRY HITS .... 00699884 / $16.99
VOL. 77 – BLUEGRASS .... 00699910 / $15.99
VOL. 78 – NIRVANA .... 00700132 / $16.99
VOL. 79 – NEIL YOUNG .... 00700133 / $24.99
VOL. 80 – ACOUSTIC ANTHOLOGY .... 00700175 / $19.95
VOL. 81 – ROCK ANTHOLOGY .... 00700176 / $22.99
VOL. 82 – EASY ROCK SONGS .... 00700177 / $17.99
VOL. 84 – STEELY DAN .... 00700200 / $19.99
VOL. 85 – THE POLICE .... 00700269 / $16.99
VOL. 86 – BOSTON .... 00700465 / $16.99
VOL. 87 – ACOUSTIC WOMEN .... 00700763 / $14.99
VOL. 88 – GRUNGE .... 00700467 / $16.99
VOL. 89 – REGGAE .... 00700468 / $15.99
VOL. 90 – CLASSICAL POP .... 00700469 / $14.99
VOL. 91 – BLUES INSTRUMENTALS .... 00700505 / $17.99
VOL. 92 – EARLY ROCK
        INSTRUMENTALS .... 00700506 / $15.99
VOL. 93 – ROCK INSTRUMENTALS .... 00700507 / $16.99
VOL. 94 – SLOW BLUES .... 00700508 / $16.99
VOL. 95 – BLUES CLASSICS .... 00700509 / $15.99
VOL. 96 – BEST COUNTRY HITS .... 00211615 / $16.99
VOL. 97 – CHRISTMAS CLASSICS .... 00236542 / $14.99
VOL. 98 – ROCK BAND .... 00700704 / $14.95
VOL. 99 – ZZ TOP .... 00700762 / $16.99
VOL. 100 – B.B. KING .... 00700466 / $16.99
VOL. 101 – SONGS FOR BEGINNERS .... 00701917 / $14.99
VOL. 102 – CLASSIC PUNK .... 00700769 / $14.99
VOL. 103 – SWITCHFOOT .... 00700773 / $16.99
VOL. 104 – DUANE ALLMAN .... 00700846 / $17.99
VOL. 105 – LATIN .... 00700939 / $16.99
VOL. 106 – WEEZER .... 00700958 / $14.99
VOL. 107 – CREAM .... 00701069 / $16.99
VOL. 108 – THE WHO .... 00701053 / $16.99
VOL. 109 – STEVE MILLER .... 00701054 / $19.99
VOL. 110 – SLIDE GUITAR HITS .... 00701055 / $16.99
VOL. 111 – JOHN MELLENCAMP .... 00701056 / $14.99
VOL. 112 – QUEEN .... 00701052 / $16.99
VOL. 113 – JIM CROCE .... 00701058 / $17.99
VOL. 114 – BON JOVI .... 00701060 / $16.99
VOL. 115 – JOHNNY CASH .... 00701070 / $16.99
VOL. 116 – THE VENTURES .... 00701124 / $16.99
VOL. 117 – BRAD PAISLEY .... 00701224 / $16.99
VOL. 118 – ERIC JOHNSON .... 00701353 / $16.99
VOL. 119 – AC/DC CLASSICS .... 00701356 / $17.99
VOL. 120 – PROGRESSIVE ROCK .... 00701457 / $14.99
VOL. 121 – U2 .... 00701508 / $16.99
VOL. 122 – CROSBY, STILLS & NASH .... 00701610 / $16.99
VOL. 123 – LENNON & McCARTNEY
        ACOUSTIC .... 00701614 / $16.99
VOL. 124 – SMOOTH JAZZ .... 00200664 / $16.99
VOL. 125 – JEFF BECK .... 00701687 / $17.99
VOL. 126 – BOB MARLEY .... 00701701 / $16.99
VOL. 127 – 1970s ROCK .... 00701739 / $16.99
VOL. 128 – 1960s ROCK .... 00701740 / $14.99
VOL. 129 – MEGADETH .... 00701741 / $17.99
VOL. 130 – IRON MAIDEN .... 00701742 / $17.99
VOL. 131 – 1990s ROCK .... 00701743 / $14.99
VOL. 132 – COUNTRY ROCK .... 00701757 / $15.99
VOL. 133 – TAYLOR SWIFT .... 00701894 / $16.99
VOL. 134 – AVENGED SEVENFOLD .... 00701906 / $16.99
VOL. 135 – MINOR BLUES .... 00151350 / $17.99
VOL. 136 – GUITAR THEMES .... 00701922 / $14.99
VOL. 137 – IRISH TUNES .... 00701966 / $15.99
VOL. 138 – BLUEGRASS CLASSICS .... 00701967 / $17.99

VOL. 139 – GARY MOORE .... 00702370 / $16.99
VOL. 140 – MORE STEVIE RAY VAUGHAN . 00702396 / $17.99
VOL. 141 – ACOUSTIC HITS .... 00702401 / $16.99
VOL. 142 – GEORGE HARRISON .... 00237697 / $17.99
VOL. 143 – SLASH .... 00702425 / $19.99
VOL. 144 – DJANGO REINHARDT .... 00702531 / $16.99
VOL. 145 – DEF LEPPARD .... 00702532 / $17.99
VOL. 146 – ROBERT JOHNSON .... 00702533 / $16.99
VOL. 147 – SIMON & GARFUNKEL .... 14041591 / $16.99
VOL. 148 – BOB DYLAN .... 14041592 / $16.99
VOL. 149 – AC/DC HITS .... 14041593 / $17.99
VOL. 150 – ZAKK WYLDE .... 02501717 / $16.99
VOL. 151 – J.S. BACH .... 02501730 / $16.99
VOL. 152 – JOE BONAMASSA .... 02501751 / $19.99
VOL. 153 – RED HOT CHILI PEPPERS .... 00702990 / $19.99
VOL. 154 – GLEE .... 00703018 / $16.99
VOL. 155 – ERIC CLAPTON UNPLUGGED . 00703085 / $16.99
VOL. 156 – SLAYER .... 00703770 / $19.99
VOL. 157 – FLEETWOOD MAC .... 00101382 / $17.99
VOL. 159 – WES MONTGOMERY .... 00102593 / $19.99
VOL. 160 – T-BONE WALKER 00102641/ $17.99
VOL. 161 – THE EAGLES ACOUSTIC .... 00102659 / $17.99
VOL. 162 – THE EAGLES HITS .... 00102667 / $17.99
VOL. 163 – PANTERA .... 00103036 / $17.99
VOL. 164 – VAN HALEN: 1986-1995 .... 00110270 / $17.99
VOL. 165 – GREEN DAY .... 00210343 / $17.99
VOL. 166 – MODERN BLUES .... 00700764 / $16.99
VOL. 167 – DREAM THEATER .... 00111938 / $24.99
VOL. 168 – KISS .... 00113421 / $17.99
VOL. 169 – TAYLOR SWIFT .... 00115982 / $16.99
VOL. 170 – THREE DAYS GRACE .... 00117337 / $16.99
VOL. 171 – JAMES BROWN .... 00117420 / $16.99
VOL. 172 – THE DOOBIE BROTHERS .... 00119670 / $16.99
VOL. 173 – TRANS-SIBERIAN
        ORCHESTRA .... 00119907 / $19.99
VOL. 174 – SCORPIONS .... 00122119 / $16.99
VOL. 175 – MICHAEL SCHENKER .... 00122127 / $17.99
VOL. 176 – BLUES BREAKERS WITH JOHN
        MAYALL & ERIC CLAPTON .... 00122132 / $19.99
VOL. 177 – ALBERT KING .... 00123271 / $16.99
VOL. 178 – JASON MRAZ .... 00124165 / $17.99
VOL. 179 – RAMONES .... 00127073 / $16.99
VOL. 180 – BRUNO MARS .... 00129706 / $16.99
VOL. 181 – JACK JOHNSON .... 00129854 / $16.99
VOL. 182 – SOUNDGARDEN .... 00138161 / $17.99
VOL. 183 – BUDDY GUY .... 00138240 / $17.99
VOL. 184 – KENNY WAYNE SHEPHERD ... 00138258 / $17.99
VOL. 185 – JOE SATRIANI .... 00139457 / $17.99
VOL. 186 – GRATEFUL DEAD .... 00139459 / $17.99
VOL. 187 – JOHN DENVER .... 00140839 / $17.99
VOL. 188 – MÖTLEY CRÜE .... 00141145 / $17.99
VOL. 189 – JOHN MAYER .... 00144350 / $17.99
VOL. 190 – DEEP PURPLE .... 00146152 / $17.99
VOL. 191 – PINK FLOYD CLASSICS .... 00146164 / $17.99
VOL. 192 – JUDAS PRIEST .... 00151352 / $17.99
VOL. 193 – STEVE VAI .... 00156028 / $19.99
VOL. 194 – PEARL JAM .... 00157925 / $17.99
VOL. 195 – METALLICA: 1983-1988 .... 00234291 / $19.99
VOL. 196 – METALLICA: 1991-2016 .... 00234292 / $19.99

Prices, contents, and availability subject to change without notice.

HAL•LEONARD®
www.halleonard.com

0820

RECORDED VERSIONS®
The Best Note-For-Note Transcriptions Available

AUTHENTIC TRANSCRIPTIONS WITH NOTES AND TABLATURE

00690603 Aerosmith – O Yeah! Ultimate Hits ... $27.99	00691190 Peter Green – Best of $24.99	00690426 Ratt – Best of.......... $19.95
00690178 Alice in Chains – Acoustic $19.99	00287517 Greta Van Fleet – Anthem of the Peaceful Army $19.99	00690055 Red Hot Chili Peppers – Blood Sugar Sex Magik.......... $19.99
00694865 Alice in Chains – Dirt $19.99	00287515 Greta Van Fleet – From the Fires $19.99	00690379 Red Hot Chili Peppers – Californication $19.99
00694925 Alice in Chains – Jar of Flies/Sap... $19.99	00694798 George Harrison – Anthology.......... $22.99	00690673 Red Hot Chili Peppers – Greatest Hits $22.99
00691091 Alice Cooper – Best of $24.99	00692930 Jimi Hendrix – Are You Experienced? $27.99	00690852 Red Hot Chili Peppers – Stadium Arcadium $27.99
00690958 Duane Allman – Guitar Anthology $29.99	00692931 Jimi Hendrix – Axis: Bold As Love..... $24.99	00690511 Django Reinhardt – Definitive Collection
00694932 Allman Brothers Band – Volume 1..... $27.99	00690304 Jimi Hendrix – Band of Gypsys $24.99	.... $22.99
00694933 Allman Brothers Band – Volume 2..... $24.99	00694944 Jimi Hendrix – Blues.......... $27.99	00690014 Rolling Stones – Exile on Main Street $24.99
00694934 Allman Brothers Band – Volume 3..... $24.99	00692932 Jimi Hendrix – Electric Ladyland $27.99	00690631 Rolling Stones – Guitar Anthology $29.99
00690945 Alter Bridge – Blackbird $24.99	00660029 Buddy Holly – Best of $22.99	00323854 Rush – The Spirit of Radio: Greatest Hits, 1974-1987.......... $22.99
00123558 Arctic Monkeys – AM $24.99	00200446 Iron Maiden – Guitar Tab $29.99	00173534 Santana – Guitar Anthology $27.99
00214869 Avenged Sevenfold – Best of 2005-2013 .... $24.99	00694912 Eric Johnson – Ah Via Musicom $24.99	00276350 Joe Satriani – What Happens Next ... $24.99
00690489 Beatles – 1 .... $24.99	00690271 Robert Johnson – Transcriptions....... $24.99	00690566 Scorpions – Best of $24.99
00694929 Beatles – 1962-1966 .... $24.99	00690427 Judas Priest – Best of $24.99	00690604 Bob Seger – Guitar Collection $24.99
00694930 Beatles – 1967-1970 .... $27.99	00690492 B.B. King – Anthology $24.99	00234543 Ed Sheeran – Divide* $19.99
00694880 Beatles – Abbey Road $19.99	00130447 B.B. King – Live at the Regal $19.99	00691114 Slash – Guitar Anthology $29.99
00694832 Beatles – Acoustic Guitar.......... $24.99	00690134 Freddie King – Collection $19.99	00690813 Slayer – Guitar Collection $19.99
00690110 Beatles – White Album (Book 1)....... $19.99	00327968 Marcus King – El Dorado $22.99	00690419 Slipknot $19.99
00692385 Chuck Berry $22.99	00690157 Kiss – Alive $19.99	00316982 Smashing Pumpkins – Greatest Hits . $22.99
00147787 Black Crowes – Best of $19.99	00690356 Kiss – Alive II $22.99	00690912 Soundgarden – Guitar Anthology....... $24.99
00690149 Black Sabbath $17.99	00291163 Kiss – Very Best of $22.99	00120004 Steely Dan – Best of $24.99
00690901 Black Sabbath – Best of $22.99	00690377 Kris Kristofferson – Guitar Collection $19.99	00120081 Sublime $19.99
00691010 Black Sabbath – Heaven and Hell $22.99	00690834 Lamb of God – Ashes of the Wake ... $24.99	00690531 System of a Down – Toxicity $19.99
00690148 Black Sabbath – Master of Reality ... $17.99	00690525 George Lynch – Best of $24.99	00694824 James Taylor – Best of $19.99
00690142 Black Sabbath – Paranoid $16.99	00690955 Lynyrd Skynyrd – All-Time Greatest Hits $24.99	00694887 Thin Lizzy – Best of $19.99
00148544 Michael Bloomfield – Guitar Anthology $24.99	00694954 Lynyrd Skynyrd – New Best of $24.99	00253237 Trivium – Guitar Tab Anthology......... $24.99
00158600 Joe Bonamassa – Blues of Desperation $22.99	00690577 Yngwie Malmsteen – Anthology $29.99	00690683 Robin Trower – Bridge of Sighs........ $19.99
00198117 Joe Bonamassa – Muddy Wolf at Red Rocks.......... $24.99	00694896 John Mayall with Eric Clapton – Blues Breakers $19.99	00156024 Steve Vai – Guitar Anthology $34.99
00283540 Joe Bonamassa – Redemption $24.99	00694952 Megadeth – Countdown to Extinction $24.99	00660137 Steve Vai – Passion & Warfare $27.50
00690913 Boston $19.99	00276065 Megadeth – Greatest Hits: Back to the Start $24.99	00295076 Van Halen – 30 Classics $29.99
00690491 David Bowie – Best of.......... $19.99	00694951 Megadeth – Rust in Peace.......... $24.99	00690024 Stevie Ray Vaughan – Couldn't Stand the Weather.......... $19.99
00286503 Big Bill Broonzy – Guitar Collection .. $19.99	00690011 Megadeth – Youthanasia $24.99	00660058 Stevie Ray Vaughan – Lightnin' Blues 1983-1987.......... $29.99
00690261 The Carter Family Collection $19.99	00209876 Metallica – Hardwired to Self-Destruct $22.99	00217455 Stevie Ray Vaughan – Plays Slow Blues.......... $19.99
00691079 Johnny Cash – Best of $22.99	00690646 Pat Metheny – One Quiet Night $22.99	00694835 Stevie Ray Vaughan – The Sky Is Crying $24.99
00690936 Eric Clapton – Complete Clapton $29.99	00102591 Wes Montgomery – Guitar Anthology $24.99	00690015 Stevie Ray Vaughan – Texas Flood ... $19.99
00694869 Eric Clapton – Unplugged $24.99	00691092 Gary Moore – Best of $24.99	00694789 Muddy Waters – Deep Blues.......... $24.99
00124873 Eric Clapton – Unplugged (Deluxe) ... $27.99	00694802 Gary Moore – Still Got the Blues $24.99	00152161 Doc Watson – Guitar Anthology $22.99
00138731 Eric Clapton & Friends – The Breeze $22.99	00355456 Alanis Morisette – Jagged Little Pill $22.99	00690071 Weezer (The Blue Album) $19.99
00139967 Coheed & Cambria – In Keeping Secrets of Silent Earth: 3 .... $24.99	00690611 Nirvana $22.95	00117511 Whitesnake – Guitar Collection $22.99
00141704 Jesse Cook – Works, Vol. 1 .... $19.99	00694913 Nirvana – In Utero $19.99	00122303 Yes – Guitar Collection $22.99
00288787 Creed – Greatest Hits.......... $22.99	00694883 Nirvana – Nevermind $19.99	00690443 Frank Zappa – Hot Rats $22.99
00690819 Creedence Clearwater Revival $24.99	00690026 Nirvana – Unplugged in New York..... $19.99	00121684 ZZ Top – Early Classics.......... $27.99
00690648 Jim Croce – Very Best of $19.99	00265439 Nothing More – Tab Collection $24.99	00690589 ZZ Top – Guitar Anthology $24.999
00690572 Steve Cropper – Soul Man $19.99	00243349 Opeth – Best of $22.99	
00690613 Crosby, Stills & Nash – Best of $27.99	00690499 Tom Petty – Definitive Guitar Collection $19.99	
00690784 Def Leppard – Best of $22.99	00121933 Pink Floyd – Acoustic Guitar Collection $24.99	
00695831 Derek and the Dominos – Layla & Other Assorted Love Songs .. $24.99	00690428 Pink Floyd – Dark Side of the Moon .. $19.99	
00291164 Dream Theater – Distance Over Time $24.99	00244637 Pink Floyd – Guitar Anthology $24.99	
00278631 Eagles – Greatest Hits 1971-1975 ..... $22.99	00239799 Pink Floyd – The Wall $24.99	
00278632 Eagles – Very Best of $34.99	00690789 Poison – Best of $19.99	
00690515 Extreme II – Pornograffiti.......... $24.99	00690625 Prince – Very Best of $22.99	
00150257 John Fahey – Guitar Anthology $19.99	00690090 Queen – Classic Queen $24.99	
00690664 Fleetwood Mac – Best of $24.99	00690003 Queen – Greatest Hits $25.99	
00691024 Foo Fighters – Greatest Hits $22.99	00694910 Rage Against the Machine $22.99	
00120220 Robben Ford – Guitar Anthology $29.99	00119834 Rage Against the Machine – Guitar Anthology $24.99	
00295410 Rory Gallagher – Blues $24.99		
00139460 Grateful Dead – Guitar Anthology $24.99		

COMPLETE SERIES LIST ONLINE!

HAL•LEONARD®
www.halleonard.com

Prices and availability subject to change without notice.
*Tab transcriptions only.

0720
272